Pagan Portals

Manannán mac Lir

Meeting the Celtic God of Wave and Wonder

T0127489

What people are saying about

Manannán mac Lir

Manannán mac Lir is an enigmatic and complex god and Morgan Daimler has written the first book which brings together thoroughly researched mythology and lore balanced with personal experience and ritual. I highly recommend *Pagan Portals: Manannán mac Lir* as an invaluable reference book and as an introduction to Manannán in his many guises.

Jane Brideson, Artist & Blogger at The Ever-Living Ones

Yet another fabulous book from Morgan Daimler, you will definitely need this one in your library. With her usual flair for detail and historical fact, Morgan takes an in depth look at Manannán and his roots. She delves into the mythology and correspondences but not just from an academic viewpoint, we also get to dip into Morgan's own personal experiences with this fascinating deity. With plenty of myths and stories to get your teeth into this book also gives some suggestions and direction to explore and connect with Manannán yourself. High recommended.

Rachel Patterson, author of several books on Witchcraft including *Pagan Portals: The Cailleach, Animal Magic* and *Witchcraft into the Wilds*

Morgan Daimler's many books on Celtic deities have been both well-researched and well-written. Morgan's current short volume on Manannán is no different. Morgan offers great information on Manannán's history and mythology, with suggestions for those wishing to honor him in different ways. The books are always an immense pleasure to read and filled with high quality material, and this volume is no exception. Highly recommended!

Erynn Rowan Laurie, author of Ogam: Weaving Word Wisdom

i

Morgan Daimler has a gift for weaving the scholarly with the spiritual, the personal with the prophetic, and does not disappoint with Manannán. The book takes you to the heart of the magnificent sea God, so that you can feel the very salt on your soul. This highly intelligent but accessible book belongs on the shelves and nightstands of lovers of Celtic myth. Now, pay for the book.

Courtney Weber, author of *Brigid: History, Mystery, and Magic of the Celtic Goddess*

Pagan Portals
Manannán mac Lir

Meeting the Celtic God of Wave
and Wonder

Morgan Daimler

Winchester, UK
Washington, USA

First published by Moon Books, 2019
Moon Books is an imprint of John Hunt Publishing Ltd., No. 3 East Street, Alresford
Hampshire SO24 9EE, UK
office1@jhpbooks.net
www.johnhuntpublishing.com
www.moon-books.net

For distributor details and how to order please visit the 'Ordering' section on our website.

Text copyright: Morgan Daimler 2018

ISBN: 978 1 78535 810 4
978 1 78535 811 1 (ebook)
Library of Congress Control Number: 2018945649

A CIP catalogue record for this book is available from the British Library.

Design: Stuart Davies

Printed and bound by CPI Group (UK) Ltd, Croydon, CR0 4YY, UK

We operate a distinctive and ethical publishing philosophy in
all areas of our business, from our global network of authors to
production and worldwide distribution.

Contents

Other Books by Morgan Daimler

Fairies
Fairycraft
Travelling the Fairy Path
Where the Hawthorn Grows

Pagan Portals
Odin
Brigid
The Dagda
The Morrigan
Irish Paganism
Fairy Witchcraft
Gods and Goddesses of Ireland

This book is dedicated to four people who equally and in their own ways have shown me Manannán's face through the mists of mortal earth: Gemma McGowan, Lora O'Brien, Erynn Laurie, and Sean Harbaugh. Go raibh maith agaibh, mo chairde. Also a huge thank you to J. T. Mouradain, Eva Thyle, Diana Hunt, and A. J. Nelson for helping me track down some pop-culture Manannán references.

Preface

The Celtic gods have often held a place, as in paganism, as one of the more popular and more often written about pantheons, yet it can be a challenge to find information on any single deity beyond the basics. Part of this is because of the simple fact that 'Celtic pantheon' is a misnomer and what we find in many books under that heading is actually a mish-mash of deities from different Celtic cultures that have been lumped together. From a historic perspective there never was a cohesive pantheon of the Celts, nor for that matter a cohesive group of people called Celts either. Instead there was a loose grouping of cultures that shared similar cultural and linguistic roots that scholars decided to label 'Celts'. Deeper inquiry reveals that these individual cultures grouped together under the Celtic umbrella tended to have shared mythic themes but very different myths and deities. In most cases as a person seeks to explore a specific deity this makes things easier because rather than a multitude of cultural expressions, we have only to seek a single one; however there are a few pan-Celtic deities, that is those who appear in some form in all or many of the so-called Celtic cultures. Manannán mac Lir is one of these pan-Celtic deities and like Brighid or Lugh – also pan-Celtic deities – it makes his story more complex and interesting to study.

Pagan Portals: Manannán mac Lir was written as a resource for seekers of Manannán, focusing primarily on the god as he appears in Irish mythology but also looking at him through other cultural lenses. This book offers both solid academic material and practical advice on connecting with him in a format that is meant to be accessible and designed to be easy to read. Like my other Pagan Portals books, it seeks to find a balance between academic references and personal interpretations as well as between older mythology and modern experiences. It is meant to be a basic introduction to this deity to help beginners become more comfortable as they seek to learn about this mysterious and magical God.

In writing this I have drawn on many different sources and have carefully referenced and cited all of them. My own degree is in psychology, so I prefer to use the APA method of citations. This means that within the text after quotes or paraphrased material the reader will see a set of parenthesis containing the author's last name and date the source was published; this can then be cross references with the bibliography at the end of the book. I find this method to be a good one and I prefer it over footnotes or other methods of citation which is why it's the one I use. I have also included endnotes in some places where a point needs to be expanded on or further discussed but where it would be awkward to do that within the text itself. I hope that this format will be useful to readers throughout.

While this book can and does serve as a stand-alone work, its ultimate purpose is to act as a first step in getting to know Manannán or to aid in deepening a relationship with him. It would be impossible for any single book to fully explore who Manannán is and obviously a book of this length could never do more than touch on his depth and significance. To make this book as useful as possible for readers to move forward in connecting further to this complicated deity, I have provided a list of both the references I used in my writing and also of recommended further reading at the end of the book under the bibliography. I have tried to offer books which represent an array of options for people, with different viewpoints and approaches to honouring Manannán. There is not a great deal of material on the market focused on Manannán and when he appears in modern books it is often as an entry in a larger work on either the Irish deities or the Celtic ones in general. I encourage readers to research the original myths for themselves and to read several translations, when possible, to get the best feel for the older stories in which he appears.

As I have said before in my previous book *Pagan Portals: The Morrigan*, I do not think that the religious framework we use to connect to the gods matters as much as the effort to honour the old gods itself. I think we can all do this respectfully and with an appreciation for history without the need for any particular religion. Whether we are Reconstructionists, Wiccans, or Celtic pagans all that really matters is that we are approaching our faith with sincerity and a genuine intention. To that end this book is written without any specific spiritual faith in mind, beyond polytheism, and it is up to the reader to decide how best to incorporate the material. My own personal path is rooted in witchcraft and reconstruction so that is bound to colour some of my opinions in the text, however, so the reader may want to keep that in mind.

I have been an Irish-focused pagan since 1991 and have long held a deep respect for Manannán. Although he is not one of the primary gods I honour, he is an important one and it has not escaped me that I was born less than a mile from the ocean and have never in my life lived further than a dozen miles away from the shore.

For some people this book may be the beginning of a lifelong journey, the first attempt to reach out to this important and complex God. For others, this book may provide a greater understanding of Manannán, his history, and modern beliefs and practices associated with him. For others, perhaps, this will simply be one piece of a larger puzzle, as I hope that those who have already spent years or decades with Manannán can still find some value here. In any case I hope that the reader feels that some value is gained from the time spent with this little volume, getting to know Manannán.

Chapter 1

Who Is Manannán?

Manannan mac Lir from the lake,
eagerly he sought for an abundance
Oirbsen his name, after hundreds of battles
death snatched him.
Lebor Gabala Erenn

One of the deities that can be found in the mythology of several different Celtic nations is Manannán; called Manannán mac Lir (son of the sea) in Ireland, and Manawydan to the Welsh. He had many powers and qualities, but for the Irish and Manx he was above all a god of the sea and today he is still often viewed primarily as the Celtic god of the ocean. His mythology and folklore was complex, however, and digging deeper we quickly find that there is much more to Manannán than waves and sea-mist. To begin, though, we will look at his name and its meaning, the basics of who he was to the Irish, Welsh, and Manx, and what his family relationships can tell us about him.

In much of his folklore his home was said to be the Isle of Man, called Manaw in Welsh and Manu in Irish; Manannán's name is derived from this. A translation of his name might be 'born of the Isle of Man' with Manann being the accusative form of Manu and the final án a common diminutive (Sims-Williams, 2011). Unlike other Irish deities then, Manannán's name would not at first seem to give us any great insight into his nature, simply reinforcing his origin, but in earlier periods the Isle of Man itself was seen as nearly mythic rather than a physical place. We may understand one layer of his name then as something like 'he who is from a mythic or Otherworldly place', giving us our first hint of who Manannán was.

4

It is likely that what is usually understood as his patronym, 'mac Lir', is actually an epithet as we know from mythology that his father's name was Allot; by this view, mac Lir is meant as a reference to his skill as a sailor and dominance over the sea (Sims-Williams, 2011). So rather than being called literally the son of Lir,[1] meaning a person, it is instead referencing the older Irish word ler, the sea or ocean, making him Manannán son of the sea. He is also sometimes known as Manannán mac Allot or Allod, a reference to his father in the mythology. According to other stories his real first name is Oirbsiu, possibly relating to the idea of flooding, although MacKillop suggests that this is an epithet rather than a first name (Macalister, 1944; MacKillop, 1998).

Since the name we now have for the Isle of Man is a later development, O hOgain suggests that Manannán himself and his mythology are later developments as well, likely dating to no earlier than the third century CE (O hOgain, 2006). One theory suggests that the Irish initially borrowed the name from the Welsh, but then added the title 'mac Lir' which was then borrowed into the Welsh as 'map Llyr' (O hOgain, 2006). This demonstrates the composite nature of Manannán that has developed over time as the cultures shared mythology back and forth. To the Manx, he was the first king of the Island of Man and stories locate his grave there, as well as tell of how he would walk among the Manx fishermen as they repaired their nets (Monaghan, 2004).

Manannán was originally said to live on the Isle of Man, a place as mentioned which was seen as near mythical in Irish stories; later his home shifted fully into the Otherworld, to Emhain (O hOgain, 2006). The Irish described Emhain in rich detail as a sacred place, an island held up by four silver legs or pillars, on which grew magical apples which gave the island the full name of Emhain Abhlach, Emhain of the Apples (O hOgain, 2006). Other names for his domain include Mag Meall [the pleasant plain] and Tír Tairngire [the land of promise] (O hOgain, 2006). Each of these names and associations reflect the connection between Manannán's realm and the Otherworld.

To the Irish he was seen as the lord of the waves, to whom the ocean was like a field of solid land, as well as a master magician and God who could control the weather (O hOgain, 2006). He appears throughout four of the major Irish mythic cycles: the Mythological Cycle, the Fenian Cycle, The Cycle of Kings, and the Imramma stories. His roles in these tales vary from minor to major and from benevolent to antagonistic.

In the Mythological cycle, although he was not counted among the People of Danu in stories until the tenth century, it is Manannán who advises the Tuatha de Danann to take up residence in the sidhe, and he who assigned each new home (O hOgain, 2006). Additionally, he gives three gifts to the Tuatha de: the féth fiadha, the feast of Goibhniu, and the pigs of Manannán (O hOgain, 2006). The féth fiadha was either a spell or cloak that allowed the person to become invisible and travel unnoticed. The feast of Goibhniu was a magical feast that kept the gods young and living. And the pigs of Manannán were immortal swine who could be killed and would return to life. Some sources suggest that it was these actions that earned him a place among the Tuatha Dé Danann, however, I believe that it is more likely that he fills a role as an outsider deity, not fully part of the People of Danu nor fully separate but liminally placed. Even his realm which is a land that is not part of the land reflects this idea.

Manannán's appearance is described as that of a handsome warrior (Berresford Ellis, 1987). One eighteenth-century story describes him fairly thoroughly this way:

A very beautiful, prosperous warrior, the most beautiful of the children of Adam was on the back of a boat with a purple fringed mantle and with a shiny silk cloak and with a variegated golden tunic and with a delightful golden sword in his possession and a bright, royal crown holding and fastening his beautiful wavy hair, protecting his shapely, fair noble head.

(Imtheacht an Da Nonbhar aus Toraigheacht Taise Taoibhghile)

We may assume this beatific description is his true one, however, in many of his appearances in the Fenian cycle he disguises himself in extremely oafish or even grotesque appearances. As the Bodach an Chóta Lachtna he appears to Fionn mac Cumhail as a giant with enormous feet, a muddy skirt, drab coat, and is described as 'thick boned' and with yellow skin (O Grady, 1892). In the stories of Ceithearnach Caoilraibhach he appears wearing pants with a narrow striped pattern on them, an old, ragged cloak, boots with holes in them and with a scabbardless-sword at his waist (O hOgain, 2006). In the story of Cormac's Golden Cup, while in disguise, he is described as a grey haired warrior wearing a golden-threaded shirt, purple fringed mantle, and white bronze shoes; later he shows his true form as a beautiful warrior.

Manannán's nature is as mercurial as the sea. When visiting Elcmar at his sidhe he is paid great tribute with rushes laid out before him and a great feast prepared, yet despite the pleasant visit he dislikes Elcmar and acts against him later (O hOgain, 2006). In the stories of the Fianna Manannán is often helpful yet also appears at least once to stir strife and create trouble among the warriors (O hOgain, 2006). This could reflect the knowledge of all sailors that the favour of the sea is fickle and quick to change, or perhaps Manannán's own liminal nature tends toward changeability.

Some sources consider him a shapeshifter, and he often appeared in disguise when travelling among mortals. Interestingly, although clearly depicted in an anthropomorphic form in stories he implies in the Imramm Brian meic Ferbail that his human appearance is a shape he is putting on saying 'This shape, he on whom thou lookest; Will come to thy parts' and 'For it is Manannan, the son of Lír; From the chariot in the shape of a man' (Meyer, 1895).

His magical powers were numerous, both in what he could

7

do through his own actions and what he could do with his many magical tools and possessions. He could travel faster than the wind could blow in his magical boat, he could create realistic illusions, and he could alter people's destinies with his cloak (O hOgain, 2006). According to myth, Manannán was killed in Connacht during the battle of Cuillenn at the hands of the warrior Uillend Faebarderg (Macalister, 1944). He was buried in Connacht as well and at the site of his grave a lake burst forth.

Manannán's Family

When we look at Manannán's family we find a tangle of contradictions and possibilities. The same source may state that his father is one person, then immediately give another possible father in the following sentence. In the same way, a goddess may be listed as his daughter or his wife depending on what story we are reading. In this way his genealogy and relations become as hazy as the famous mist he was said to conjure to help hide the Tuatha Dé Danann when they travelled on mortal earth, and we must look at this section as possibilities rather than certainties.

Manannán was the son of Allot according to the Lebor Gabala Erenn (LGE) although the Coir Anmann lists his father as Allaei. It is possible that this is an example of a scribal error between different texts. In an alternate genealogy in the LGE, however, his father is said to be Elcmar. His mother is never named; according to the Lebor Gabala Erenn he had two brothers, Bron and Ceti, each of whom had a plain named after them. According to the Altram Tige Dá Medar, the Dagda was his foster father. Allot is the Dagda's brother according to the LGE which would make the Dagda Manannán's uncle and a logical choice as foster-father; it would also firmly anchor Manannán amongst the Tuatha De Danann. However, while sources do list him as a son of Allot son of Elada, and later writers, including the author of the Leabhar Breathnach Annsis So, state that he is the Dagda's nephew; he is

8

also said to be the son of Allot son of Alathan which would give him a different paternal grandfather than the Dagda and imply that the Allot who was his father was a different figure. That would tally better with his usual distinct position as an outsider among the Tuatha Dé. Ultimately there is no clarity on the issue. There are many stories about his various sons and daughters, who are usually treated as minor characters (O hOgain, 2006). For example, two of his daughters, Glina and Monoge, gave their names to lakes in Galway but little else is known about them. In the Altram Tige Dá Medar we are told that one of his sons was named Echdrond Mor and his daughter was Curcog. According to the LGE, his sons are Gaiar and Orbsen, although Orbsen may also be another name for Manannán himself. In 'The Adventures of Art son of Conn' we are told that his sons are Ilbrec and Gaidiar (possibly synonymous with Gaiar). A description of Manannán's foster son Lugh in one text also includes a reference to 'the sons of Manannán' who are named as: Scoith Gleigeal, Rabhach Slaitin, Gleigeal Garbh, Goithne Gorm-suileach, Sine Sindearg, Domhnall Donnruadh, and Aodh mac Eathaill[2] (MacQuarrie, 1997). A more extensive list of his children compiled from the Lebor Gabala Erenn and Tochmarc Luaine adds sons Cairpri, Failbi, and Gaela to this list and daughters Gormlinde, Niamh, Grian, Comand, Muinfind, Tamann, Crofind, Tibir, and Uaine (MacQuarrie, 1997). One of his more well-known children is Áine, although some sources say that she was the daughter of his foster-son Eoghabhal (O hOgain, 2006).

It is said that Manannán travelled to the mortal world to father Mongán, a prince and hero, and under the name of Oirbsiu he may have fathered the Conmhaicne sept of Leinster (O hOgain, 2006). He seems to have an active interest in the mortal world and didn't hesitate to interfere directly when it seemed necessary to him, as we will see in his mythology.

Additionally, Manannán may be the foster father of several important deities. According to one myth he is the foster-father of the Dagda's son Aengus, who he raises and also advises, helping

Aengus to gain possession of his home at Sid in Broga [Newgrange]. He may also be the foster-father of the God Lugh and of Fer I and Eogabal (Smyth, 1988; MacKillop, 1998). In wider folklore and stories he is known to take on a similar role with heroes and kings and act as their teacher.

Manannán's wife is Fand, a peerless beauty who at one point had an affair with Cu Chulain, until Manannán used his magic to make Cu Chulain forget about her and return to his own wife, Emer. In the *Echtra Cormaic meic Airt*, Fand is described as the most beautiful woman on earth. Alternately in some folklore his wife is said to be Áine, although as already mentioned she may be his daughter instead. In one myth we are told that Manannán's wife is named Uchtdelb but that he falls in love with Áine and his wife with Áine's brother Aillén, resulting in the married couple trysting with the siblings (Williams, 2016). In some folklore local to the Beara peninsula[3] it's said that Manannán was the lover of the Cailleach, and that she turned to stone waiting for him to return to her. In the stories of the conception of Mongan, his lover is the mortal woman Caintigern, the wife of Fiachra who Manannán fathers the king, Mongan, on.

In the Lebor Gabala Erenn, Manannán is said to be killed by Uillen, son of Eochu Garb, although later folklore attributes his death to Ullin son of Tadg son of Nuada Argetlamh (Macalister, 1944; Todd, 1892). When he died in battle in Connacht, a lake burst forth from his grave, originally called Loch nOrbisu but later known as Loch Corrib (O hOgain, 2006). Manx lore places his grave on the Isle of Man. As with all the Irish deities it is worth remembering that death is not a permanent situation for the gods and no matter how often they ae killed in stories they always seem to reappear again later.

Manannán in My Life

I have an interesting relationship with Manannán. For me, most other gods are beings that I had to find one way or another. I came

10

to witchcraft and Irish paganism in my pre-teens and immediately started researching the Irish gods, beginning my worship with Danu, the Dagda, and to a lesser extent, Brighid. Later I would come to respect and honour Macha and the Morrigan and eventually Badb and Nuada. But my relationship with the ocean and its God is complex.

I was born within less than a mile of the Atlantic Ocean and have lived my entire life – no matter where I've moved to – within no more than a dozen miles from the shore. I have an instinctive affinity for selkie stories because I understand what it's like to feel that both the sea and land are a part of you, to feel torn between the two.

But when I was seeking deities to worship I didn't look to ocean gods because I have always been ambivalent about the ocean and its power. Some people fear storms, or fire, or madness – all purviews of other gods. What I feared was the deep bottomless depths of the ocean, the places where ships disappear and where sharks live. The white capped waves which are as deadly as they are beautiful. I loved the ocean the way I loved breathing but I also feared it because I knew that as much as it gives it also takes. And to me there is no difference between the ocean and the deity who rules the ocean.

Over time, though, I began to see that my fear was born of a desire to control what cannot ever be under mortal control. And the more I started to see that it was my fear of being without control that was the root of my fear, the more that fear shifted to respect. I still know the power of the ocean and I understand its mercurial nature – but I also think I have come to know the importance of the lessons it teaches, both when it is mild and when it is fierce.

Only with this growing respect did I begin to grow closer to the deity who rides across the waves. Finally I was ready to reach out to Manannán and see what he could teach me.

11

Endnotes

1. Manannán is certainly not the son of Lir, father of the children of Lir from the story Oidheadh Chloinne Lir. There is nothing in mythology connecting Manannán and that Lir to each other and there is some speculation among scholars that Lir himself was a later literary creation rather than a being from genuine older tradition.

2   I'm a bit sceptical of Aodh mac Eathaill, since he is being called Aodh son of Eathaill, but with the others we are given first names and epithets, many of which relate to colours which is interesting.

Scoith Gleigeal, scoith [maybe a form of scoit, liquid] gleigeal glé clear geal bright

Rabhach Slaitin, rábach bold, fruitful slaitin small rod

Gleigeal Garbh, gleigal bright-clear garb rough

Goithne Gorm-suileach, goithne small dart gorm-suileach blue-eyes (although gorm has multiple meanings)

Sine Sindearg, ancient storm-red

Domhnall Donnruadh domhnall red-brown

3. I have no written references to this but have heard it in several places now, and saw it mentioned in relation to the Cailleach Beara stone in Beara. It is clearly modern folklore, but has gained enough traction to have attached itself to the site, so I am offering it here for the reader's consideration.

Chapter 2

Irish Mythology

In Irish literature he appears mostly as King of the Fairies in the Land of Promise, a mysterious country in the lochs or the sea. His character seems to have been a most contradictory one – many tricky actions are ascribed to him, while he was very strict about other people's morality. At his court no one's food would get cooked if, while it was on the fire, any one told an untrue story, and he is said to have banished three men from fairy-land to the Irish court of Tara for lying or acting unjustly.

Rys, Hibbert Lectures, 1886

Manannán appears often throughout various Irish mythological texts, sometimes with an essential role and sometimes only tangentially. All of these appearances are important however in giving us a better understanding of who Manannán is and the different powers he wields, as well as the various gifts he has and can bestow on people.

In this chapter, which will likely be the heaviest in this book, we will look at many of the texts in which this enigmatic deity appears, although I am by no means claiming that this list is exhaustive. I have tried to include the most important stories that I am aware of and will recap them so that readers can get a sense of their importance and Manannán's role within them. I encourage everyone to read the myths in full for themselves, and to be aware that in recapping them here, I am including only the highlights that focus on Manannán's roles and leaving out, in some cases, a great deal of important but unrelated story material.

Lebor Gabala Erenn

The Lebor Gabala Erenn (LGE) is a series of books which describes the successive invasions of Ireland by different mythic beings, ending with the arrival of the Gaels. Volume four in the series looks at the Tuatha De Danann and Manannán appears in several places. The LGE, however, is less of a prose work as we would understand it today and more a collection of listed facts and short poetic sections, and it also comes to us today in multiple versions, called redactions, which can at times be contradictory. This can sometimes make the text off-putting for modern readers and somewhat difficult to work through. It is still a useful book for learning details about the various members of the Tuatha De Danann and in this case Manannán is listed in at least three places with biographical details that give us insight into who he is.

The first section in the LGE that mentions Manannán tells us that he is the son of Allot and has two brothers, Bron and Ceti, both of whom have plains named for them in Ireland. We also learn that he is a 'chapman[1] who was [trading] between Ireland and Britain' and that he recognized the 'dark or the bright signs in the air' (Macalister, 1944). Beyond the genealogical information this is interesting because it tells us that Manannán was known for his travelling and also for his ability to read the signs in the air. We may interpret this as meaning either an ability to navigate by the stars or to read omens in the sky; it might even reference astrology or something similar although that is purely speculation.

The next section discussing Manannán says:

Manannan mac Lir from the lake,
eagerly he sought for an abundance
Oirbsen his name, after hundreds of battles
death snatched him. (Macalister, 1944)

Manannán is associated with lakes in more than one source, with the next passage in the LGE also telling us that he has a lake – as well as a plain – named for him. His connection with water more generally, both freshwater and saltwater, is ubiquitous and this is only one example of that. Here, we are also told that another name for Manannán is Oirbsen[2] and that he was killed after 'hundreds of battles' implying that he was a skilled warrior.

The next section of the text to mention him reiterates several points made in the last, mentioning that 'Orbsen' may have been his other name and that he died in battle. However, here we are also told that he had two sons, Gaiar and Orbsen, the second of which may or may not have been another name for Manannán himself. This passage in the LGE states that two places, Loch Orbsen [lake Orbsen] and Mag Orbsen [plain of Orbsen] were both named for Manannán based on the belief that Orbsen was indeed his other identity. Finally the LGE tells us that Manannán met his death in battle in Connacht, in the battle of Cuillenn, at the hands of a warrior named Uillend Faebarderg.[3] It should be kept in mind, however, that the Irish gods are often said to die in myths only to reappear later having recovered from their death seemingly unscathed and retaining their original personality and character.

Altram Tige Dá Medar

One of the more interesting myths featuring Manannán is the Altram Tige Da Medar. Manannán has a key role in this story and here we see him described as a king among the Tuatha De Danann as well as a foster-son of the Dagda. Although this particular story has heavy Christian overtones it is also full of some very important information about Manannán and has deeply layered information more generally about pagan theology, particularly highlighting some of the differences between the Tuatha De Danann and the sidhe.

The story opens with the defeat of the Tuatha De Danann by the Gaels and their subsequent retreat beneath the sidhe of Ireland. Bodb Derg and Manannán are made joint kings over the Tuatha De but it is Manannán who decides where each of the gods will live now, appointing each by name to one of the sidhe. Additionally, Manannán gives the Tuatha De Danann three powerful gifts: the

Feth Fiadha, the Feast of Goibhniu, and Manannán's Swine. The Feth Fiadha was a concealment that would hide them; Goibhniu's Feast would keep them eternally young and healthy; the Swine of Manannán could be killed one day and would live again the next. Manannán taught all of this to the Tuatha De Danann so that they could live as the people of the sidhe did, and in response they declared that his law should rule over all of their homes and he should be present at every wedding and feast. Either because of this or simply by habit, Manannán regularly made a circuit to visit all the sidhe and enjoy their hospitality.

So the story goes that Oengus was the foster-son of Elcmar, and was sent out to invite Manannán to a feast at Elcmar's home of Brugh na Boinne. A great feast was prepared and all the gods attended and were envious of Elcmar's wonderful home. After three days of copious feasting Manannán spoke privately to Aengus and urged him to try to take the Brugh for his own, saying that as a foster-son of the Dagda he wished to help the Dagda's son. The story then includes a passage of Christian theology, wherein Manannán is supposedly teaching Aengus about the one true God, but while this is probably the result of later Christian insertion it does include what may be older pagan themes. For example, Manannán encourages Aengus to tell Elcmar to leave the Brugh until 'ogham and pillar be blent together, until heaven and earth, sun and moon be blent together' (Dobs, 1929).

Manannán successfully convinces Aengus to trick Elcmar from the Brugh, and all of Elcmar's people go with him save only his steward and the steward's family who were not at the Brugh at the time. Aengus asks the steward to remain on and pledges to raise the steward's unborn child as his own foster-child, along with any child of the Tuatha De Danann. Manannán's wife is also pregnant and so Manannán accepts this offer as well and agrees to put his child in Aengus's care. The steward's wife gives birth to a daughter named Eithne and Manannán's wife to a girl named Curcog; the two are raised together and become close friends.

Later, Eithne is insulted by Aengus's brother and stops eating or drinking, able only to drink milk from a particular dun cow out of one specific golden goblet. When Manannán becomes aware of this he attempts to use all of his magical skill to get the girl to eat again, to no avail, finding that when she visits him with his daughter she can only consume the milk of one of his speckled cows. Finally he declares that the reason she cannot eat is because she belonged neither to the Tuatha De Danann nor the sidhe but that when she had been insulted her magic and her guardian daemon had left her and an angel had come in its place. Because she claimed then by the Christian God she could not eat the food of the Tuatha De Danann but only from the cow that was brought from India because that was a 'righteous land'.

Manannán, of course, speaks truly, and it comes to pass that Eithne is eventually lost to the Tuatha De Danann. She wanders from her companions at the Brugh after a time when clerics have come into Ireland and is found by a priest who takes her in. Aengus searches for her, but she chooses to stay with the Christians and dies a fortnight later, to the great grief of her foster-father and Curcog.

Serglige Con Culain

A story that belongs to the Ulster Cycle, the Serglige Con Culain tells the tale of Cu Chulainn hunting birds which turn out to be Otherworldly beings. He finds himself unable to strike the birds and that night dreams of two Otherworldly women, one clad in green the other in red, who beat him unmercifully with horse-whips.

Cu Chulainn then falls into a wasting illness for a year until a strange man appears to him and tells him that the two women he is seeing are the man's sisters, Liban and Fand, and that Fand wishes to marry Cu Chulainn. He promises that if Cu Chulainn agrees he will be healed of the illness from which he is suffering. Cu Chulain goes back to the same place he first saw the women and speaks to the green clad woman, who identifies herself as Liban. She swears they meant him no harm but that her sister was Manannán's wife until he abandoned her, and that the women had grown to love Cu Chulain; they came so that Fand could marry him and Liban could gain his help for her husband Labraid, in a day's fighting. There is some communication back and forth between Liban and Cu Chulainn, and through the medium of Cu Chulainn's charioteer; eventually Emer finds out that her husband's illness is due to fairy women. She encourages him to throw off such enchantment but he seems at least somewhat interested in Fand's offer.

However, he changes his mind on meeting Fand in person and goes with her, fighting for Labraid and spending a month with Fand in Mag Mell. They return together to Ulster, and when Emer finds out what has transpired she goes with 50 maidens armed with knives to avenge her honour. Instead of a physical fight, however, Emer and Cu Chulainn end up in a verbal fight that ends with both women insisting the other should be the one to keep him. This comes to Manannán's attention and he goes to retrieve his errant wife, appearing hidden to mortal sight so that only Fand can see him. Fand recites a long poem about her relationship with Manannán describing their relationship. She begins by pointing out the sea god only she can see, calling him 'lord over the world's fair hills' and saying that there was a time he was dear to her and that if he were to be loyal to her even then she would return his affection. She laments that they should ever have been parted, claiming that she was a worthy spouse to him, that he could not win against her at chess, mentions the gold bracelet he gave her as a courting gift. She talks about her coming across the sea, and then again says she sees Manannán 'the horseman of the crested wave' coming to them, without the need of ships, invisible to anyone except the fairy-folk.

Manannán arrives and Fand leaves with him, but Cu Chulainn and Emer are so distraught by the incident that King Conchobar has his druids make them both drinks of forgetfulness, so that neither one remembers Fand or the events with the fairy women. Manannán also shakes his cloak between Cu Chulainn and Fand to ensure that neither will ever meet the other again.

Tochmarc Etaine

Manannán gets a passing reference in the Tochmarc Etaine where we are told that it is he who kills Midhir and Fuamnach at Brí Leith, Midhir's stronghold, although other versions say that it was not Midhir he killed but Midhir's grandson Sigmall (Leahy, 1906).

Tochmarc Luaine

A story from the Ulster cycle that is focused on King Conchobar finding a wife, the Tochmarc Luaine also tells us of a character named Manannán son of Athgno who attacked Ulster during this time to avenge his foster sons who Conchobar had killed. The text tells us that:

There were four Manannáns, and not at the same time were they.

Manannán son of Allot, a splendid wizard of the Tuath dé Danann, and in the time of the Tuath dé Danann was he. Orbsen, now, (is) his proper name. 'Tis that Manannán who dwelt in Arran, and from him Emain Ablach is called, and 'tis he that was killed in the battle of Cuillenn by Uillenn of the Red Eyebrows, son of Caither, son of Nuada Silverhand, contending for the kingship of Connaught. And when his grave was dug, 'tis there Loch n-Oirbsen broke forth under the earth, so that from him, the first Manannán, Loch n-Oirbsen is named.

Manannán son of Cerp, king of the Isles and Mann. He was in the time of Conaire son of Etirscél, and 'tis he that wooed Tuag daughter of Conall Collamair, Conaire's fosterson, and from her Tuag Inber is named.

Manannán « son of the sea », to wit, a famous merchant who traded between Erin and Alba and the Isle of Mann. He was also a wizard, and 'tis he was the best pilot who was frequenting Ireland. 'Tis he too that would find out by heavenly science (i.e.) by inspecting the air, the time there would be fair weather or storm, ...

Manannán son of Athgno was the fourth Manannán. 'Tis he that came with the great fleet to avenge the sons of Uisnech, and 'tis he that had supported them in Alba. (Stokes, 1903)

Looking at this, however, the first three listed Manannáns, while distinct in some ways, also seem to be overlapping to such a degree that they can easily be seen as the same deity appearing in different guises. While the final Manannán may be a unique character, scholars do tend to treat Manannán mac Allot, Manannán who was king on the Isle of Man, and Manannán mac Lir as one cohesive being with divergent mythology. This is not difficult to believe because Manannán does show up in various disguises throughout mythology as is evident in other examples in this chapter, including the next story.

Echtra Bodach an Chóta Lachtna

A story from the Fenian Cycle where we see a figure called the 'Bodach an Chóta Lachtna'[4] who scholars believe is Manannán in disguise. In some alternate versions he identifies himself as such at the end of the tale.

In the story Fionn and his Fianna are near the shore when they see a great warrior approach in a boat. He tells them that he is Cael in Iarnach [possibly 'Slender the Fetters'] the son of the king of Thessaly and that he has travelled around the entire world putting all the places he visits under tribute to his father, so that they all must pay a tax. He has now come to Ireland to do the same, and challenges a single man of them to beat him in a race, sword fight, or wrestling match. Fionn realizes that none of his warriors, including himself, are capable of defeating Cael but they are honour-bound to try to defend Ireland. He buys time by saying he must go and fetch Caeilte who is their best runner and leaves to go in search of him.

On the way he meets a stranger, a giant of a man strangely dressed and wearing a grey coat. The stranger convinces Fionn to tell him of his troubles and then proclaims that only he can save Ireland from Cael. When Fionn asks the stranger his name he replies 'Bodach an Chóta Lachtna'.

Although Cael does not want to race against the ugly and loutish Bodach, he agrees to a race of 60 miles and the two set off to a point that distance away from the place they are all in, planning to run back to the group of Fianna the next day. When the two arrive, the Bodach suggests they build a house to stay the night but Cael refuses, saying he would do no such thing with the rough Bodach, so the Bodach builds a stout house out of timbers himself. He then asks Cael if the other would join him in hunting for dinner and again the other refuses, so the Bodach hunts a boar himself, then raids a house many miles away to get plates and wine, then returns and consumes half the boar himself and a cask of wine. When the morning arrives and Cael wakes him to begin the race, the Bodach refuses saying he hasn't slept enough, then sleeps another hour while Cael begins running. The Bodach gets up, eats the other half of the boar, drinks another cask of wine, before finally setting off, running as fast as birds fly and quickly catching up to Cael. He mocks the other man and suggests he run faster if he really wants to put Ireland under tribute. He passes Cael and runs ahead only to stop and eat blackberries by the wayside. Cael eventually reaches him and tells him that he has lost the two skirts of his coat many miles back. The Bodach says that to be fair Cael should wait there for him to go back and retrieve them, but Cael refuses. So the Bodach runs swiftly back, retrieves the cloth, sews them back to his coat, then catches back up to Cael without any effort and passes him again. He stops to pick more blackberries, this time filling his coat with them before heading off to win the race. When he arrives among the Fianna he asks that they give him an amount of grain equal to the blackberries he has brought to eat while they wait for Cael. As he is eating they finally see the king's son approaching, furious and ready to do battle. The Bodach flings a handful of grain and blackberries at him and knocks his head around to the back of his body, then lunges at him, drives him to the ground and picks him up. He makes the prince swear by sun and moon that it will be Thessaly that will pay rent to Ireland every year as long as Cael lives and then sends him, crippled, away in his ship.

Returning to the Fianna, the Bodach tells them that he is actually a fairy – síoghaidhe – from the fairy hill of Cruachan [rátha Cruachan] who had come to aid them. In gratitude, Fionn holds a feast that lasts for a year and a day for the fairy-man.

Duanaire Finn

The Dunaire Finn is possibly our best source for the story of the Crane Bag, one of Manannán's most important possessions, although, during this story it has come into the hands of Fionn mac Cumhal, through his father. Poem 8 tells how the goddess Aoife was cursed into the shape of a crane by a woman who was jealous because they both loved the same man, Manannán's son Ilbrec. In this form, Aoife was doomed to live for 200 years in the house of Manannán, unable to leave or return to her true shape. When Aoife died, Manannán took her crane skin and used it to make a magical pouch to hold a variety of treasured objects. This crane-bag then passed to other owners before returning again to Manannán, eventually being given to Fionn's father Cumhal.

Imram Brian mac Ferbail

In this story we see the adventures of Bran son of Ferbal outlined, beginning with the appearance of an Otherworldly woman bearing a silver apple branch. She recited 50 verses to Bran describing Emain Abhlac. The woman disappeared, taking the silver branch with her, but Bran was inspired by her words to take a company of men the next day and head off on a sea voyage.

As he crossed the ocean he saw a man coming towards him in a chariot who said he was Manannán, going to Ireland to father Mongan. Manannán recited 30 verses of a poem to this effect, describing how, to him, the sea that Bran perceived was a smooth plain, the waves were flowers, and the fish were cattle and sheep. He told Bran that he would go to Ireland and father a great king and warrior, someone he would train, mentioning that Mongan would be able to take many animal forms and that although his life would be relatively short, he would be renowned. He also said that when Mongan was finally fatally wounded a fairy host would be sent to bring him to the Otherworld.

The two then part and Bran goes on to visit the Land of Women, and Otherworldly Isle. After a time his men become homesick and he is urged to return to Ireland, however, when they get back to the shore they find a great amount of time has passed and they are all the stories told by old men. One of his men leaves their boat and turns to dust upon touching the earth; Bran tells of all their adventures to the man on land, then he and his company turn and leave for the open ocean.

Echtra Airt meic Chuind

Manannán has a small part at the beginning of this story.

Manannán's son Gaidiar has an affair with another man's wife, Becumla, and the Tuatha Dé Danann are gathered to judge what punishment she will have for the transgression. Manannán and two of his sons, Gaidiar and Ilbrec, as well as several others are part of this judgement but when it is decided that she should either be banished or killed, it is Manannán who says it would be better to banish her. He tells the others that if she is killed her guilt may become part of the land or of the people, so banishing is better. Becumla is then banished to Ireland, with all of the fairy-mounds of Ireland closed to her. She goes to Ireland and causes great trouble and misery there to King Conn and his son Art.

Echtra Cormaic maic Airt

Manannán appears to King Cormac one day, disguised as an old man carrying a silver branch bearing golden apples; when the branch shook it made a delightful noise. Cormac asked the old man about it and was told it came from the Otherworld where there were no lies nor ageing nor sadness. The king was so enamoured of the sound that he was willing to give anything in trade for it. The stranger said he would give it to Cormac if Cormac would promise him three forfeits later. Cormac quickly agrees in order to get the coveted magical branch.

Once he has it he returns to his court at Teamhair and shows the gathered people the branch; shaking it for them, he casts them all into a magical sleep that lasts for a full day.

A year later the stranger appears at Cormac's court and requests the first forfeit – that he be given Cormac's daughter Ailbe. Cormac hands over the girl to the dismay of his court but after the stranger has disappeared with her he shakes the apple branch and they all forget their sorrow. The following month the stranger appeared again demanding his second forfeit – Cormac's son Carpre. Again everyone was lost in grief until Cormac shook the magic branch. The stranger returned for the third time and for his final forfeit he took away Cormac's wife Ethne.

This time, though, Cormac couldn't stand the loss and he gathered warriors about himself to pursue the stranger. As they travelled, a wall of white mist closed around them and passing through it Cormac found himself alone on a wide plain. Moving on he saw a fortress behind a bronze wall. Inside was a house thatched with white birds' wings and a troop of fairy horsemen with armfuls of bird wings perpetually thatching the house which had its roof blown off by the wind so that their work never ended. Inside the house was a man burning an oak log.

He moves on to another bronze-walled fortress, this one containing four houses. These houses are also thatched with white bird wings, and are built from bronze and silver. Inside the fortress walls Cormac sees the fairy troop drinking from a fountain that is the source of five musical streams whose sound is more pleasant than people singing. Around the well grow nine hazel trees[5] and as the hazel nuts fell into the water they were eaten by five salmon swimming in the fountain.

Cormac enters a palace in this fortress and sees a couple there, a beautiful warrior and a golden haired woman wearing a gold helmet. He finds a small room with a bath where the heated stones for the water go in and out of the bath themselves and he washes. He returns to the main room and joins the couple and shortly thereafter a man comes in with a pig and a large oak log. The warrior tells the man to prepare a meal for their noble guest so he kills the pig and quarters it, then chops the log up, preparing the fire and setting the pig in a cauldron. However, Cormac is told that each quarter of the pig will only cook if a truth is told for it. The three Otherworldly beings take turns telling true stories and three-quarters of the pig cooks; for his portion Cormac tells of his meeting the stranger and gaining the apple branch and then his adventures until that point. The food being cooked, Cormac is urged to eat but refuses saying he will not eat unless there are 50 people in his company, so the warrior puts him into a magical sleep; upon waking he finds himself in such company and his wife and children among them. The warrior hands him a golden cup and says that if three lies are told the cup will break into three pieces but three truths will restore it. He demonstrates by lying to break the cup but the truths he tells to repair it are that Cormac's wife and daughter have been kept safely in no contact with any men since being taken from him and his son likewise, and in no contact with any women. He then gifts the cup to the king and gives him back his family, declaring that he is in fact Manannán mac Lir and that all was done to bring Cormac to the Land of Promise. He explains each thing that Cormac has seen since crossing through the mist and tells him that when Cormac dies the cup and branch will return to Manannán.

Compert Mongáin

A complicated story in which we see Manannán directly interfering in the world of humans. First, the king of Ulster, Fiachna the Fair is drawn into battle with the king of Lochlann over a broken promise for which Fiachna had agreed to act as surety.[6] When Fiachan leads his army against Lochlann they find themselves facing venomous sheep that kill 300 men each day. On the fourth day Fiachna himself decides to go out and fight, even if it means his death, but he is stopped by the arrival of a mysterious warrior who promises to take care of the venomous sheep in exchange for the gold ring on Fiachna's finger and a night of sex with his wife. The strange warrior promises that a son will be born of this union and then identifies himself as Manannán mac Lir. Fiachna agrees and Manannán produces from beneath his cloak a venomous hound to kill the venomous sheep.

The son, named Mongan, is born and Manannán takes him when he is three days old to live in Emhain Abhlach not bringing him back until he is sixteen years old. By that point Fiachna the Fair has been killed by his rival Fiachna the Dark, but when the boy is returned the people decide that the kingdom of Ulster should be divided between them and that Fiachna the Dark's daughter Dubh-Lacha [black duck] should marry Mongan. Later Manannán goes to Mongan disguised as a dark haired priest and convinces Mongan to rise up and kill Fiachna the Dark.

Mongan then goes on to enter into a bad bargain with the king of Leinster that costs him his wife in exchange for 150 white red-eared cattle that he wanted. He falls into a wasting sickness over her loss and uses the magic that he learned from Manannán, specifically of disguise and of love magic, to eventually win her back again.

Compert Mongáin (alternate version)

There is an alternate version of the story of Mongan's conception which has a very different view of what happened. In this story

Manannán went to Fiachna's wife, while he was away fighting in Scotland, and told her that her husband would die the following day in battle with a great warrior. He said that if she would have sex with him he would go and save her husband's life by defeating the warrior, and she would conceive a son who would grow to be famous. She agreed and Mongan was conceived; Manannán kept his word and went to the battle and saved Fiachna's life, helping his army to win the battle besides. Afterwards he told Fiachna what had happened and that he had been sent by Fiachna's wife to aid him. When Fiachna returned to Ireland he found his wife pregnant and she did indeed give birth to a son who was known as Fiachna's but also Manannán's. The story is clear, by the way, that Fiachna thanked his wife for what she had done to save him. The story ends with the wife relating a quatrain Manannán had said before he had left her, where he identifies himself as Manannán and says that he is returning to his home.

Ceithearnach Caoilriabhach

A sixteenth-century story that is seen in many different iterations, where a soldier in disreputable attire, including striped pants, holey shoes, a tattered cloak, and a sword with no scabbard, travels around visiting various lords and acting both offensively and helpfully. Some versions explicitly state that this figure was Manannán in disguise 'because he used to be this visiting everyone as a trickster' although O hOgain is sceptical and suggests that this assertion is simply an assumption based on Manannán taking on that role in other tales (O hOgain, 2006).

Cóir Anmann

The Cóir Anmann is a collection of names and descriptions compiled during the late medieval period. Although it is a later source, and it was assembled piecemeal over a period of time, it does offer us insight into how a variety of mythic figures were viewed and understood at the time. The entry on Manannán is particularly interesting as it both attempts to paint him as a human with special skills and knowledge and also describes him as a God of the sea. The author seems to waiver between euhemerization and acknowledgement of his divinity. The passage is short so I will include it in translation below:

156: Manannán mac Lir that is Oirbsin his name. Oirbsiu was his proper name Allaei the name of his father. That is a wonderful trader who was on the island of Man that is he was the best steersman on the sea in the west of the world. He knew through understanding, as it was actually written, through sky knowledge, that is through gazing at the appearance of the sky that is the air, the length of the world, the fine weather or stormy weather, and when the two elements would change each other, and the people of Britain and the men of Ireland called him the God of the sea and Mac Lir he was called that is son of the sea. Manannán moreover he was called for the Isle of Man. (Daimler, 2015)

Sanas Cormaic

The Sanas Cormaic was a text attempting to offer etymologies for a variety of Irish terms and is considered one of the earliest attempts at such. Most of the etymologies in the text are what we would consider folk etymologies rather than actual legitimate ones but they can still offer insight into the views on the words and concepts at the time. In the case of Manannán, Cormac can show us what view was held about him in the later Middle Ages. The original text is written in both Sengoidelc and Latin, a not uncommon blend in some of the source material. Since it is short I'll include the entirety here:

Manannan mac Lir, that is a famous trader from the Isle of Man. He was the best navigator in the sea in the west of the world. He used to tell through meteorology, that is the form of the skies, that is through inspecting the sky, the length there was the good weather and the time it changes to the other kind. The Irish and British called him a god of the sea and then the son of the sea that is 'mac lir', and the name of the Island of Man was called for Manannán. (Daimler, 2018)

Manannán in My Life

My favourite story of Manannán is probably the Altram Tige Dá Medar, although Manannán's role in that story is convoluted. I like, though, that it challenges me to really think about who Manannán is, not just in himself but also in relation to the Irish gods. Is he one of them? Is he something unique?

I like to see him acting as a lord of the Sidhe though clearly separate from the Tuatha De Danann and I enjoy the idea that it was Manannán who taught the Irish gods how to live as the aos sidhe did, hidden from human sight and immortal in our world. It paints him in a fascinating role as both separate from but also acting on the side of the Tuatha De Danann and there is something about that dichotomy that fascinates me. Yet as the story goes on it seems clear, to me, that he is also a part of the Tuatha De Danann as well, intrinsically woven into their family structures and tuath [tribe or people]. He is the classic outsider but he is also just as much an insider and that very liminality has an allure for me.

Manannán is a being who has his own kingdom in Emhain Abhlac, his own people and his own distinct and impressive power, yet here we see him acting as one of the Tuatha De Danann, advising them on where to live in their new homes among the fairy hills and teaching them how to thrive there. He even gives them three gifts, all of which represent essential powers for the Tuatha De to possess in order to maintain their prominence now that they are in the sidhe.

His actions initially seem entirely benevolent and yet then we see him encouraging Aengus to deceive Elcmar in order to win the Sid in Broga, in an act that seems pointlessly harsh. Certainly in the story it upsets both Elcmar and ultimately Aengus as well. Yet Aengus owning the Sid in Broga seems to be a vital thing, something we see emphasized in many different stories, and so perhaps we could see a deeper meaning to Manannán's actions here. Maybe he isn't merely acting maliciously against someone he dislikes, as he seems to dislike Elcmar, but rather moving with a larger motive. Just as he moves to aid Fiachna as part of a wider plan to conceive a child with Fiachna's wife Caintigern, knowing that child will be an important and powerful mortal king, we can see greater wisdom and wider vision in all of Manannán's actions.

His stories have shown me that he takes the long view, even the extremely long view, and acts in ways that will prove good in the end even if the immediate actions seem unpleasant.

Endnotes

1. A Chapman is a kind of trader or travelling salesman. The idea here then is that Manannán is a traveller between the different areas of Ireland and Britain.

2. The etymology of Oirbsen and Oirbsiu is uncertain as far as I know. I find it interesting, however, that the name bears at least a resemblance to 'orb' and 'sen' which together could be read as 'ancient inheritance'. That is purely speculative as it stands, however, it resonates for me with Manannan's nature.

3. There are several things of particular interest about this section: 'Uillend Faebarderg s. Eochu Garb s. Dui Temen, by him was Manannan slain in the battle of Cuillenn in Connachta' (Macalister, 1944). Cuillenn appears to be a form of the word cuilenn, a name for the holly tree. The name of Manannan's opponent translates to 'Honeysuckle Red-bladed son of Rough Horse son of Dark Fool'.

4. The word lachna means both grey or milk-white but when applied to clothing, as in this case, probably refers to unbleached wool.

5. There has been some suggestion that this well is the same

as the Well of Segais or Well of Nechtan, however, I tend to disagree. While the description does bear surface similarities there are also differences, for example, the location. Also the other two wells had specific prohibitions relating to who could drink from them while this one clearly does not. Manannán in the story explains the fountain as the 'Fountain of Knowledge' and the source of the five sense which are the five streams, and says that all people of art and wisdom drink from it.

6. Basically, Fiachna had promised to ensure that both parties kept their word in an agreement. In this case the king of Lochlann needed a specific red-eared white cow from a witch named the Cailleach Dubh, but she did not want to do this. He offered to give her four cows in return but she didn't trust him so she only agreed if Fiachna would promise to see that the king's word was kept.

Chapter 3

Outside Ireland

... the people of Britain and the men of Ireland called him the God of the sea and Mac Lir he was called that is son of the sea. Manannan moreover he was called for the Isle of Man.

Coir Anmann

The bulk of the material covered in this Pagan Portal focuses on Manannán as an Irish deity, however, he does appear under very similar names in related Celtic cultures, particularly the Welsh and Manx. While the Irish material is more abundant, we can learn about who Manannán was and is by looking at his cognates in these other cultures, their mythology, and how they were understood by those cultures.

Wales

To the Welsh Manannán – or more properly Manawydan – was a skilled craftsman and trickster deity (O hOgain, 2006). He appears in the Mabinogi although his character here is markedly different from the Irish Manannán and has, at best, a tenuous connection to the ocean. Instead what we see in the Welsh mythology is a deity who is skilled in a variety of trades, who offers good counsel, who is clever and observant, and has strong connections to enchantment.

While the Irish Manannán had a brother named Bron, the Welsh Manawydan had one named Brân vap Llyr (Sims-Williams, 2011). There is some speculation that the Irish Bron and Welsh Brân may be the same personage, however, not enough is known about Bron to be certain.

In Welsh myth, Manannán as Manawydan appears in the second and third branches of the Mabinogi as well as in some later poetry. He is a pivotal character and also related to important characters, including the goddess Rhiannon. In the second branch of the Mabinogi, Manawydan is presented as the brother of Brân the Blessed who is the king. In this story he is clearly an important character, sitting next to his brother Brân at the wedding of their sister Branwyn to the king of Ireland, Matholwch and sent by his brother to Matholwch to apologize when their other brother offends the Irish king. Later in the story they find out that their sister is being mistreated by her new husband and go to war to rescue her, resulting in the deaths of all but seven of the rescue party. Manawydan survives but his brother Brân is mortally wounded and requests that his head be removed and placed so that it can watch over and protect the land. During the journey home, with Brân's animated head keeping them company, they stop in an enchanted castle where they feast and forget their sorrows; Manawydan realizes that opening a specific door in the castle will break the enchantment but does not do so. Finally, though, another of their companions opens the door and they all remember their grief and continue home. Brân's head is buried where it will protect the land.

In the third branch, Manawydan is accompanying Pryderi, the son of the goddess Rhiannon, on the return from Ireland after the previous story has left off. Since Manawydan has no land of his own, Pryderi invites him to join him in his own home of Dyfed. However, after marrying Rhiannon the land falls under an enchantment and all of the people and livestock disappear except for Manawydan, Rhiannon, Pryderi, and his wife Cigfa. The group make their way by hunting and working as craftsmen but are continuously driven from place to place as their skill is greater than anyone else's and they inspire jealousy everywhere they go. Eventually they return to the still-enchanted Dyfed. There Pryderi is lured into a mysterious fort by a white boar and disappears. When Manawydan tells Rhiannon of her son's disappearance she is angry with him and goes to rescue Pryderi herself, only to disappear as well. Manawydan and Cigfa attempt to go and work as craftspeople but are again forced to return to Dyfed. When they return this time, Manawydan plants three fields of wheat. To his dismay two of the fields are stripped of produce so he carefully guards the third and sees it being attacked by mice. He manages to catch one of the attacking rodents and declares that he will hang it as a thief. Three different people appear in turn to beg clemency for the rodent but Manawydan is adamant that it will be hung. The third stranger asks him what he would accept in exchange for the mouse's life and Manawydan says he will take nothing less than the return of Rhiannon, Pryderi, and the removal of the curse on Dyfed. This is done and it is revealed that the curse was placed by Llwyd in revenge for Rhiannon spurning his friend's suit[1] and marrying Pryderi's father instead. The mouse Manawydan captured was Llwyd's pregnant wife.

Manawydan is also mentioned in several Welsh poems as one of King Arthur's knights where he is associated with both giving good counsel and being a powerful warrior (Green, 2007). In the Trioedd Ynys Prydein he is named as one of three premier shoemakers in Wales (Jones, 2003).

Isle of Man

Manannán in the Isle of Man is in some ways similar to what we have seen in the Irish, and much of the Manx material references directly or repeats Irish mythology. In Man he is called Mannanan beg mac y Leir or 'little Manannán son of Leir'; the name is cognate to his other forms in Ireland and Wales. MacQuarrie suggests that Mananan beg might be read as 'dear little Mananan'.

One source describes him as the first king to hold the island, a man who could through necromancy raise a concealing mist and who could make one man look like a hundred to defend against enemies (Todd, 1892). In both the Isle of Man and western Ireland it was said that Manannán travelled with his magical mist, moving on three legs that rolled like a wheel; the three-legged wheel which is the Manx emblem may come from this (Smyth, 1988).

Manannán's place in Manx lore is a bit ambivalent with few references to him in folklore that do not clearly reflect Irish influence or older Irish material. It is difficult to say then whether he began in Man and was exported out or began in Ireland and was imported in. As with later Irish folklore of Manannán though, which will be touched on in Chapter 6, Manx folklore holds that it was a Christian saint that drove the pagan God out to the island's detriment. The poem 'Mannanan Beg, Mac Y Leir, ny Slane Coonty Jeh Ellan Vannin' claims that Saint Patrick forced Manannán out of the Isle of Man resulting in a loss of blessing and prosperity for the island (MacQuarrie, 1997).

One Manx storyteller when interviewed in 1983 said of Manannán:

I have heard the old people say that Mananan beg mac y Leir was once upon a time king of Man. They used to say he was yellow in colour and would go in the form of three legs and roll over Man from one end to the other like a huge wheel ... (MacQuarrie, 1997)

In almost all of Manannán's mythology, across cultures, he was said to have originated on the Isle of Man or to rule from there with the physical location in the mortal world having an Otherworldly reputation. He was particularly associated with South Barrule, a hill in the south of the Isle of Man which contains the remains of an old fort; folklore says that this place belonged to Manannán and that he ruled from here when he was king.

Stories variously say he was a God later euhemerized into a man, or a man later thought of as a God. In either case he was viewed as a powerful magic worker and protector of the Isle of Man. One story claims he averted a Viking invasion by fashioning a fleet of small boats out of sedge then enchanting them to look like warships; the invaders were so frightened by the sight of the apparently fierce warships that they turned and fled (Manannán mac Lir, 2018).

Every midsummer the people of Man were said to pay rent to Manannán – or Mannanan beg – in the form of rushes (Morrison, 1911). This rent not only allowed them to live on the island but also ensured Manannán's protection. The offering of rushes can be interpreted in various ways and has been called rent, a tax, and an offering in various places. It is possible that this yearly formal offering reflects an older ritual practice that has largely been lost (MacQuarrie, 1997).

Manannán – by that name – appeared in a 1917 poem by Mona Douglas 'Vision of the King'. The poem depicted Manannán among a 'faery' host riding across the Isle of Man. He stops and speaks about the unconquerable nature of the island and its people and his eternal rulership over it. His fairies respond by declaring that he is indeed king of all the island and that the old spirit of the land would rise again. It ends with Manannán and his host returning to their land and the narrator who witnessed this declaring the spirit of the Isle of Man re-awakened.

The poem is usually viewed as political in tone and an appeal to Manx independence. This is in line with the wider political climate at the time, and the pressure that the First World War was placing on the Isle of Man to separate from the UK (Richardson, 2017). However, this also demonstrates the way that Manannán continued to be a powerful symbol for the Manx even into the twentieth century and reaffirms his place as divine king and owner of the island.

A fisherman's prayer from the Isle of Man to Manannán asks for his protection and blessing on their efforts and travel:

Manannan Beg Mac Lir –
Little Manannan Son of the Sea,
Who blessed our island,
Bless us and our boat, going out well.
Coming in better, with living and dead[2] in our boat.

Traditional fisherman's prayer (Manannan mac Lir, 2018)

Scotland

Manannán is not found much in Scotland, however, Alexander Carmichael does note in his Carmina Gadelica a healing charm for urine issues, 'Eolas Bun Deirg 181' which calls on Manannán surreptitiously in a later verse:

The nine wells of Mac-Lir,
Relief on you to pour
Put stop to your blood
Put run to your urine
You cow of cows, black cow
Great sea,
Red cascade,
Stop blood,
Flow urine.

Carmichael also compares Saint Michael to the Neptune of Gaelic culture, likely a veiled reference to Manannán (Williams, 2016).

Manannán is also referenced in two poems in the early sixteenth-century work 'The Book of the Dean of Lismore'. In the first poem the poet is bemoaning the slowness of his doctor in attending to him and claims he would gladly give several valuable items, if he could, to cure his illness; he includes among these items 'the herds and flocks of Manannán' (MacQuarrie, 1997). A later poem in the same book references the sows of Manannán and 'a horse and mare of the fine stud of Mananan' (MacQuarrie, 1997).

Manannán in My Life

One of the most reassuring things to me about Manannán is the way he is associated with both specific locations like the Isle of Man and also the entire ocean which is his place. I can stand on my own shoreline, my feet in the Atlantic Ocean here in America, and know that these are still his waters in some sense. Just like I know this ocean is the same ocean that touches the shoreline of Ireland even though I can't see it. It's a connection that means a lot to me and there have been times when I have really needed that sense of his presence in the waves and mist, even here in New England.

I have also found comfort in the knowledge that Manannán has a certain quality that is both rooted and rootless. He is strongly tied to certain places and his stories often take place or reference places in our world that can be seen or visited. We can go to Loch nOirbsen, where it's said Manannán is buried or to south Barrule and see the ruins of the place he was said to rule from on the Isle of Man. Yet at the same time he is as fluid as water, shifting from Ireland to Wales to Man, and carried perhaps even further by those who call on him. Scholars do not know where he began or even why his name is what it is, and yet across millennia and cultures people still find power and meaning in his stories.

Wherever I am and wherever I find my feet standing, I still feel as if Manannán is nearby, in the mist and ocean waves.

Endnotes

1. These events occur in the first branch of the Mabinogi.
2. Dead here is likely a reference to the fish that have been caught.

Chapter 4

Items, Animals, Possessions, Places and Holy Days

He had a silver branch with three golden apples upon his shoulder. There was so much pleasure and entertainment, moreover, in listening to the music which the branch made, so that wounded men, or women in labour, or sick warriors would fall asleep to the music the branch made when he shook it.

Echtra Cormaic meic Airt

Manannán has a wide array of associations in mythology and folklore to different items, animals, possessions, and was known for his connection to one holiday in particular. In this chapter I want to take a look at these associations and the deeper symbolism we can find within them. I think that we can gain a better understanding of who Manannán was and is through learning about the things that are around him and which belong to him.

Items

There are a few general items that are either associated with Manannán or were said to belong to him but which he gave, or possibly taught, to others.

Reeds – In one version of the story of the Taking of the Sidhe where Manannán is the king over the Tuatha De Danann he is greeted by reeds laid out on the ground to welcome him. Similarly, in the Isle of Man reeds are offered at midsummer as the rent of the people to Manannán. The reed may be a particularly ideal offering, as a plant which grows in both salt and fresh water, for a deity who is associated with both the sea and lakes. Although referred to in sources as reeds, the actual plant involved is likely a variety of the Juncus [Irish Luachra] or rushes of some type (MacCoitir, 2012).

They were traditionally used to thatch houses and strewn on floors as a sign of hospitality (MacCoitir, 2012).

Féth Fíadha – Possibly the same thing as Manannán's magical cloak [see below] but in a more general sense. Understood to be either a magical mist or else a magical cloak or garment that disguises both the Tuatha De Danann and some druids from mortal sight. Manannán taught the féth fíadha to the Tuatha De Danann when they retreated into the sidhe so that they could pass unseen when they travelled in the mortal world. Some sources would seem to make this a tangible, wearable object, for example, in stories like the Altram Tige Dá Medar we see a person's ability to be concealed by the Féth Fíadha failing when a garment described as a veil is lost. In other cases, however, the Féth Fíadha is clearly described as a spoken charm or prayer, such as we see in Saint Patrick's lorica. MacKillop compares it directly to the ceó druídechta, the druid's fog and suggests the name means 'lord's fog' from féth, fog or mist, and fíada, lord or master (MacKillop, 1998).

Apple Branch – In the story of his meeting with King Cormac mac Art, he is described as carrying a silver branch with golden apples that rang with sweet music that could soothe people to sleep or heal the ill and wounded (O hOgain, 2006). Similarly, the Otherworldly woman he sends to Bran in the Imramm Brain meic Ferbail arrives bearing a silver apple branch. MacQuarrie suggests that the apple branch itself may be a symbol or tool of passage to the Otherworld.

Animals

Manannán has a selection of animals in general that are associated with him as well as several specific ones. The fish are said to be his livestock, compared to cows and sheep, and he is sometimes said to have magical birds and hounds (MacKillop, 1996). Manannán also had three cows, one red, one white, and one black who lived beneath the water but emerged once to walk on land (Beveridge, 2014).

There is a folktale from 1835 which features Manannán interfering in a horse race, where he defends the honour of an Irish family challenged to a race by an Englishman by appearing in human guise and offering to race the English horse himself (MacQuarrie, 1997). Of course the God wins, to the shock of the Englishman. This is possibly an echo of the story where he aided Fionn by racing the prince of Thessaly but it also puts him in the same category with other horse deities who were renowned for being swifter than horses themselves, including Macha and Áine. It should also be noted that the waves are called the horses of Manannán and that his Welsh counterpart Manawydan marries Rhiannon, a horse goddess, creating multi-layered connections between Manannán and horses.

Manannán also has a connection to birds through the crane bag and his centuries-long care for Aoife in her crane form. Beveridge, in the book *Children into Swans*, also suggests that as a shape-shifter, Manannán could assume the form of sea birds in general and heron specifically.

Aonbharr – His special horse is Aonbharr, which O'hOgain gives as Enbarr meaning 'water foam'[1] who could run over sea as if it were solid land (O hOgain, 2006). Aonbharr is sometimes borrowed by other people in stories, understandable since she was said to be able to run as fast as the wind blew and no one riding her could be struck down. She can also run over water as easily as land, crossing the ocean as another horse would cross a plain. In mythology she is described as dark grey and in at least one passage of the Acallamh na Seanorach as wearing a golden bridle (MacQuarrie, 1997).

Swine of Manannán – One of the three gifts that Manannán gave to the Tuatha De Danann when they entered the sidhe; the swine were pigs who could be killed and would be alive the next day. The idea of pigs, in particular, that could be killed and resurrected is seen in other tales as well including the Fate of the Children of Tuireann and descriptions of the Brugh na Boinne. It is possible that these pigs were part of the feast of Goibhniu and were essential to the immortality of the Tuatha De Danann (Williams, 2016). If this view holds true then the pigs are not only immortal themselves in that they can be killed and live again the next day but they also convey the same quality to those who consume them.

Possessions

Manannán has a wide array of possessions said to belong to him although when we see them appearing in stories they are sometimes in the hands of other mythic figures. Lugh in particular is said in several stories to have something specific belonging to Manannán, which makes sense since Manannán is his foster father.

Magical Cloak – Manannán was said to have a magical cloak in the Serglige Con Culain, and he used this cloak to ensure that two people would never find each other again. Some modern sources say that this cloak causes forgetfulness but this seems to be a confusion between the cloak which Manannán used, s the story says: 'Manannan shook his cloak between Cuchulain and Fand, to the end that they should never again meet' and the drink which Conchobar had his druids fashion and give to Emer and Cu Chulainn so they would forget the incident (O'Curry, 2009). The cloak has the colours of the sea and shines in the light (MacKillop, 1998).

Cup – Manannán possessed a magical cup which would break in portions if a lie was told in its presence but would mend itself should the truth be told (MacQuarrie, 1997). This cup was given to King Cormac during his lifetime but returned to Manannán after Cormac's death.

Armour – Manannán has a set of special armour: a coat of mail, a breastplate and a helmet. No one wearing these items can be injured (MacQuarrie, 1997). He also possessed a shield, which like many of his treasures, passed through the hands of other gods and human heroes and returned to him. The shield was made out of wood from a tree that had been infused with poison dripping from Balor's severed head after the Cath Maige Tuired, although it's unclear if this gave it any special properties.

Crann Buide – The 'yellow tree', a spear or javelin said to belong to Manannán but seen in possession of Diarmuid in the story Toruigheacht Diarmada agus Grainne. In the story we see Diarmuid using the spear to complete a feat of arms that cannot be duplicated (Cross & Slover, 1936). It is worth noting that Diarmuid is the foster son of the god Aengus, himself likely the foster son of Manannán, possibly explaining Diarmuid's possession of the Crann Buide.

Frecaid – Called 'the Answerer'[2], this is Manannán's sword and as with all his possessions it has some very special qualities. He wore it on his left side, showing that he was right handed[3] and it was said that anyone injured by it would die from the wound and that if it were drawn in battle anyone who saw it would be as weak as a woman in childbirth (MacQuarrie, 1997).

Móraltach – Another sword attributed to Manannán is Móraltach which appears in the story of the Tóraigheacht Dhairmada agus Ghráinne. It was said to leave no mark when it struck a person. In the story the sword has been given to Naoise and his brothers by Manannán and in the end is used is to strike a simultaneous blow, at Naoise's request, so that all three brothers can die together.

Corr Bolg – The Crane bag may be one of the most famous of Manannán's possessions and one that over time also belonged to other famous people including Fionn mac Cumhal's father. It was made from the skin of his son Ilbrec's lover, Aoife, who had been transformed into the shape of a crane by a jealous rival. When she died, Manannán used her skin to fashion the crane bag, a magical item that filled and emptied with the patterns of the tide. According to the Dunaire Finn, the Corr Bolg contained: Manannán's shirt and knife [possibly the same as his chainmail shirt and sword], Goibhniu's corslet, a smith's hook, the king of Scotland's scissors, the king of Lochlann's helm, bones from Asal's pig, and a corslet made from the spine of a whale.

The Corr Bolg belonged to Manannán but then to Lugh until he was killed by the sons of Cermait Milbeol. Those three then had the Corr Bolg until they were in turn killed and Manannán reclaimed the bag, keeping it until it came into the possession of Conaire, then eventually Cumhail, Fionn's father.

Scuaba Tuinne – The boat of Manannán, the Scuaba Tuinne, or 'wave sweeper'[4] is a magical craft which would fit the description of an Irish currach. Anyone in it had only to say where they wanted to go and they would be taken there; in one story Manannán's boat is described as made of bronze (MacQuarrie, 1997). The boat was often loaned to others, but it had the special qualification that it could not be complained at, possibly because it would not work if it was ill treated (Williams, 2016).

Places

Emhain Abhlach – Emhain is probably the most well-known place associated with Manannán, and the one most commonly referenced in relation to him. The name comes from Eumania, relating to a tumulus or other sacred site and before that was likely the name for the Isle of Man itself, Manu (O hOgain, 2006). The full name includes the word 'Abhlach' giving us 'sacred place of apples'. Although clearly a specific location it is also sometimes used as a sort of generic term for the Otherworld itself and Emhain is also called by other names including Mag Mell [pleasant plain] and Tír Tairngire [land of promise] and may be related to or the same as Tír na nÓg [Land of the Young]. It is clear in all accounts that while his domain is an island, it is also the Otherworld, and as much as this one specific place belongs to him, the ocean in its entirety is also said to be his.

It is described fairly thoroughly in the *Imramm Brain meic Ferbail*; at the beginning of the story an Otherworldy woman appears to Bran and sings him 50 verses, many of which directly deal with Emhain. She describes the place as upheld by four feet or pillars made of white bronze and surrounded by 'seahorses'.

She also mentions several specific areas by name, including the southern plain of Mag Findargat where 'the hosts hold games: coracle contends against chariot' (Meyer, 1895). The island is a place without illness, unhappiness, death, deception, or infirmity. Interestingly, some of these same ideas are reflected in the way the Isle of Man is described in a sixteenth-century poem 'Mannanan Beg, Mac Y Leir, ny Slane Coonty Jeh Ellan Vannin' which says that Man is a place free of anxiety, care, or hard work. This may reflect the often ambiguous way that the actual Isle of Man and the Otherworld and Otherworldly realms were viewed.

Caiseal Mhanannáin – A real world location associated with Manannán can be found in Roscommon, Ireland, as part of the Rath Cruachan [Rathcroghan] complex. This is Caiseal Mhanannáin, or the stone fort of Manannán. The fort today is not a main attraction at the complex and is a fairly unassuming area of slightly raised earth, however, originally it would have been a triple-ringed stone fort and quite impressive to behold. One theory holds that Caiseal Mhanannáin was a defensible home for high status people during the Iron Age, while another says that it was a school for druidic teaching (Curley, 2013). The idea that the site was a druidic school is certainly a fascinating possibility and one that would link back to Manannán's role as an enchanter and wielder of magic.

Ballymannin – Located in the parish of Bekan in county Mayo, the site is now a ruin but it was once said to be the home of Manannán (CITA, 1999). There was also at one time a lake named Loch Mannin nearby, however, the lake was drained in the 1960s and no longer exists; there is some speculation that this may have been the lake which burst forth from Oirbsiu's grave (CITA, 1999).

South Barrule – His special location on the Isle of Man is the height of South Barrule. On the summit can be found the remains of a stone fort, which folklore says was Manannán's castle.

Lough Corrib – A lake in Connacht, it was said to have been formed when the water burst forth from Manannán's grave as it was being dug. Originally named Loch nOirbsen.

The Ocean – Manannán is firmly associated with the ocean both as a boatman and as someone for whom the water was like dry land. In the Imramm Brain he says that when he looks upon the ocean he sees a flowering plain where Bran sees water. It was said that Manannán could travel by going beneath the ocean for the space of nine waves then emerge on the tenth wave as dry as if he'd never touched water (O hOgain, 2006). His connection to the sea is found in both Irish and Manx mythology, and persists whether he is being described as a human, deity, or fairy.

Two different names for the waves reference Manannán, one saying they are his horses the other that they are the locks of his wife's hair (O hOgain, 2006).

Manannán's Holy Day

Midsummer has a long and complex association with Manannán, which is particularly interesting for two reasons. Firstly, we have little existing pagan lore, particularly Irish, connected to the solstices or equinoxes so the strong connection between the summer solstice and Manannán stands out. Secondly, the other Irish deity with a strong, notable, connection to Midsummer is Áine who is herself intrinsically connected to Manannán.

Manx folklore dating from at least the sixteenth century tells us that the belief was that when Manannán was the ruler over the Isle of Man, people would go on Midsummer's eve and offer him green rushes (Moore, 1891). By some accounts it wasn't the eve of the solstice but rather the night before Saint John's Eve that this was done, and there is often some fluidity in folklore between the two concepts and dates. The core concept remained the same on whatever date we believe it occurred: people had to give Manannán reeds in payment for his protection, so that they could remain living in his land.

Manannán in My Life

One of the times that I have personally felt the closest to Manannán

46

was when I was out on a whale watch trip off the Beara peninsula. We set out before noon and spent a good five hours on the ocean, looking for various sea life that is known to frequent the area, including basking sharks, seals, and minke whales.

I have spent time on boats before, as a child, but this was the first time that I had ever gone out with the intention of focusing on connecting to the water and its spirit – or spirits – in a wider sense. There is a marked difference between connecting to the ocean on the shore and doing so in the middle of its vastness and I think, for me, this experience was the first time I understood the true scope of Manannán's realm. We were fortunate that the day we went out was fair and reasonably calm but even under good conditions there is something humbling about the ocean.

We were lucky and we did see whales while we were out, we even had one surface very close to our boat. Minke whales are one of the smallest of the baleen whales yet the adults are between 20 and 30 feet long. Seeing one up close was thrilling but reinforced that we were tiny beings in a large and alien space.

Perhaps this should have been frightening but I found it just the opposite – feeling tiny and lost among the endless blue and the mysterious depths made me feel closer to Manannán and I found that closeness comforting. There was a sense of presence for me in the sun and salt and wind, a sense of not being alone. It's counterintuitive, I realize, and I don't know exactly how to explain it except to say that as we crossed the water heading out on our quest to see whatever we could find, I felt like we were not merely a group of people on boats, and when we stopped and drifted looking and waiting for the eventual reward of the whales, I felt as if Manannán was there with us as well.

In his dissertation on Manannán, Charles MacQuarrie (p. 28), says that, 'Manannan himself, as implied in his second name Mac Lir, seems to be a personification of the sea – the sea made flesh.' Sitting out on a small boat on the ocean, I felt like I truly understood those words for the first time. The sea was all around us and with the water was a feeling of presence, of awareness, of the sacred. Manannán wasn't in the waves; he was the waves. Manannán wasn't part of the ocean; he was the ocean. Looking out across the vast blue there was no difference between the mundane and the numinous.

Endnotes

1. Aonbharr doesn't literally mean water foam, however, while Enbarr means 'foam' or froth. Aonbharr is obscure but could mean something like 'unique point' or 'unique product'.

2. In Old Irish this would correctly be frecraid, however, it is often given in secondary sources with the spelling of fragarach. I suspect that this is similar to the issue we see with the variant spellings of Aonbharr, although it may also represent an Anglicization or partial Anglicization from the Irish.

3. This may seem like a minor detail, or something obvious, but I feel it's worth pointing out rather than leaving people to assume. We know that not all the Irish gods were right-handed as Nuada, for example, lost his right arm which was his shield arm in the Cét-Cath Maige Tuired indicating that he was left handed.

4. Scuaba can be read several ways but I am giving here the way it is most often translated into English, as 'sweeper'. I'd merely note that it is a form of the word scúap.

Chapter 5

Multifaceted Deity

As they were thus conversing, they saw a single tall warlike man coming towards them. He wore a green cloak of one colour, and a brooch of white silver in the cloak over his breast, and a satin shirt next to his white skin. A circlet of gold around his hair, and two sandals of gold under his feet... [he said] '... I am Manannan, son of Ler.'
Compert Mongan

One thing that we see repeatedly with Manannán is that while he is often with the Tuatha Dé Danann, even possibly one of their kings, he is not truly one of them. In several stories his status as an outsider is emphasized and often this status is predicated on his place among the people of the sidhe, who the Tuatha Dé Danann join but remain to some degree separate from. It is a reminder that Manannán is a liminal being even among liminal beings.

It is worth remembering as we contemplate Manannán's many facets and qualities that he is a mercurial deity and that whatever we can say about him will include as many contradictions as certainties. Manannán refers to himself as both sweet and sour in his actions and his mythology backs this up. As Williams describes him: 'Manannán came to personify the ambivalences which were part and parcel of the late medieval view of the Tuatha Dé Danann: his knowledge is deep, his interventions unpredictable, and his morals dubious' (Williams, 2016, p. 253).

Sea God – Manannán is generally considered the ocean god of the Celts. Although some people do debate whether Lir could also be a sea deity, as has been discussed earlier, what is often assumed to be a partonomic, 'mac Lir', is instead more likely an epithet meaning son of the sea. There are multiple references to Manannán as a premier sailor or boatman, as both a god and a euhemerized human.

He is sometimes compared or equated to Neptune or Poseidon and often depicted riding his horse across the waves (Smyth, 1988). He is also on occasion related to the Norse deity Aegir, another god of the sea (Jones, 2013). Alexander Carmichael in the Carmina Gadelica in turn may be referencing Manannán when he compares Saint Michael to the 'Neptune of the Gaels'.

He was seen as not only being masterful on the ocean but also as having control over it. In one folktale he had three sons who were arguing, Manannán became so frustrated with them as they continued to bicker that he didn't hold the tide back from the bay where they lived; all three drowned (O hOgain, 2006).

God of Magic – In many of Manannán's mythic appearances we see him performing magical acts and he has a definite connection with magic. In later folklore he was seen as both a renowned magician and also as a wise magic-worker who would teach students, for example, Galway folklore relates that youths might go to Manannán to learn magic (O hOgain, 2006). His site in Tulsk, Caiseal Manannain, is speculated by some to have been a druidic school or training location of a similar nature (Curley, 2013). A story from the nineteenth century refers to Manannán as 'the king of druidism and enchantment' and 'the best man at druidism to be found' and elsewhere he is called Aengus's tutor in druidism (MacQuarrie, 1997, p. 284). He used his magic in stories for a variety of reasons, including enchanting objects and protecting people and places. It was said in the Isle of Man that he protected the land without use of any weapons, using only his magical skill.

God of the Sidhe – Manannán is the lord of Emhain Abhlac, an Otherworldly realm, and it is clear that this was his place long before he found any role among the Tuatha De Danann. It is his very power and skill as a Fairy King that allows him to help the Tuatha De when they are defeated by the Gaels and driven into the sidhe, because Manannán already knows how to survive as one of the Hidden People. He is the one – in some stories – who divides up their new homes in the fairy hills among the Irish gods, and he is the one who teaches them how to live successfully there. He shows them how to pass unseen in our world and for all intents and purposes teaches them how to go from gods of the sky and above-world to gods of the mounds and hidden places. In later folklore, like many of the Irish gods, Manannán is himself referred to as one of the fairy folk (MacQuarrie, 1997).

Trickster God – Manannán is often referred to as a trickster deity by scholars as well as by some of his modern followers and of all the Irish gods he may best deserve the label. When we looked at his mythology in Chapter 2 there was a clear pattern of Manannán either advising others in deceitful actions or acting deceitfully himself. For example, in one version of how Aengus won the Sid in Broga as his home, it was Manannán who suggested the strategy he should use to trick the property from his foster-father Elcmar. In the story of Mongan's conception, Manannán used deceit to convince Mongan to attack his human-father's killer by appearing to him disguised as a priest. He also acts in disguise when aiding Fionn against the prince of Thessaly and when travelling around as the warrior in the striped pants. Usually his actions in disguise are helpful to those he interacts with, but not always and in some stories he causes mischief or even harm to those he visits depending on his mood.

Psychopomp – There is no historical evidence of Manannán as a psychopomp, which is a spirit who guides the dead between this world and the next. However, as we have seen, there is evidence of Manannán travelling between the Otherworld and our world and sometimes, as we see in his interactions with Cormac, guiding a person between the two. He also promises in the Imramm Brain meic Ferbail that his son Mongan will be taken by 'the white host' to the Otherworld; while this doesn't directly connect him to psychopomp activities it does relate him to the idea of sending the fairy host out to bring a soul to the Otherworld.

In truth, there is no clear psychopomp among the Irish gods, although there are several possible candidates, Manannán being one of them. Some Irish pagans choose to look to him for help when souls are passing over from the mortal world to the Otherworld and in my own experience I have seen him respond; I believe that the gods do evolve and adapt to the needs of those who worship them. It should be understood, though, that this is a modern understanding of Manannán.

God of weather – An aspect of Manannán that is probably underrated today is his ability to control or influence the weather. In folklore it was said that storms could be caused by his anger (O hOgain, 2006). This connection to weather more generally is something we see across folklore with the people of the Otherworld. His aspect as god of weather may relate to his place among the aos sidhe or it may connect back to his role as a god of the sea, as he was sometimes said to create storms by stirring up the waves (MacQuarrie, 1997).

God of Creation – Another more obscure aspect of Manannán is as a deity of creation. One argument is for Manannán as the creator of the Otherworld in particular, as manifested by his revealing of this world not only to earthly kings and heroes but also to the Tuatha De Danann themselves in some versions of how the Tuatha De move into the sidhe. MacQuarrie argues for this metaphor as a type of creation via revelation. A more direct possible creation story is hinted at in the Imramm Brain meic Ferbail where it is said that Manannán stirred the sea until it was blood which MacQuarrie sees as either a reference to Manannán creating the earth from the primordial ocean or re-enacts the creation of the world 'and thereby manifests the Otherworld' (MacQuarrie, 1997, p. 27).

Warrior – Manannán has a strong association with a variety of weapons, as we discussed in Chapter 4, both defensive and offensive. It is clear when these weapons are described in the stories that they are not only his possessions but tools that he uses. He is referenced as a teacher of warriors, and when he appears to Cormac in the Otherworld, in what may be one of his true forms, he is described as a warrior. Although many of his stories hinge on his ability to solve difficult problems, including potential invasions, through cleverness and deception he is also undoubtedly a powerful and successful warrior.

Advisor – A common theme in many tales is for Manannán to take on the role of advisor, tutor, or foster-father. He fosters Lugh in many stories, sometimes raising him on the Isle of Man and other times fully in the Otherworld; he is also by some account the foster-father of Aengus. In both cases he acts not only as a father figure to these beings but also advises them on specific and important actions to take. In the story of the Imramm Brian he tells Bran when they cross paths that he will be both Mongan's father as well as his teacher, and promises to make him a powerful magician and good king. In some folklore Manannán's advice is essential to Lugh's conception as he aids Cian in vital ways that lead to his tryst with Ethliu. Even in later folk tales we continue to see Manannán in the role of advisor and teacher, for example, a story recorded in 1932 tells of Manannán teaching the king of Ireland's son for 21 years until he can be matched in wit and martial skill by only one other person (MacQuarrie, 1997). Manannán is a wise and crafty deity but one who is willing to share his knowledge and cleverness to aid others for their own gains. As MacQuarrie puts it: 'The role of Otherworld tutor and/or to kings and heroes is certainly a traditional one and is clearly an important part of his function in the folklore and romances' (MacQuarrie, 1997, p. 286).

Manannán in My Life

Living near the ocean, I tend to feel his presence in the fog and mist, as well as sometimes in the ocean waves.

Where I live we often have heavy mist or fog, sometimes to the point of minimal visibility, and when this happens I find myself thinking of the Féth Fíadha and the magical Druidic mist. While I tend, for myself, to think of Manannán's magical cloak as an actual cloak, I can see the beauty in the metaphor of the mist as his cloak when we are walking through it and our surroundings are obscured. There is something inherently mystical and mysterious about a heavy fog that makes the numinous seem nearer, I think, and makes it easy to believe that anything is possible. I often find as well that when the mist is heavy and the world is obscured it is easy to feel as if the Otherworld is indeed only a step through the fog. And in those moments it is easy as well to see why and how the mist came to be associated with Manannán, lord of enchantment and king of the Otherworld.

Besides the beauty and power of the mist, I also perceive his presence in the power of the ocean and the waves, and the water more generally. I believe it is important when connecting to Manannán to remember the truly awesome power of the ocean and of water, both to nourish and to destroy; power that reflects and is reflected by Manannán's own personality and actions in mythology. The same ocean that feeds and comforts us can as easily kill us if we do not respect it; the river that gives us water to drink and a place to swim can rise up in a flood and destroy our homes. Manannán can bless us or harm us, and we would be wise to remember the true nature of his power as we honour him.

Chapter 6

In the Modern World

I go to my house, the clear-bright morning is at hand, it is he Manannán mac Lir, the name of the man who came to you.

Compert Mongain

Like many of the Irish gods, Manannán has survived well in the modern world, although he is often viewed now as a figure of folklore or culture rather than explicitly as a deity. Nonetheless his name remains reasonably well known and his association with the sea is still strong. Manannán was so popular, in fact, that Marian McNeill went out of her way to mention him in her book *The Festival of Lughnasa*, although she acknowledges that he plays no great role in the holiday of Lughnasa. She does, however, admit the power his name maintained into the modern period, especially in relation to the ocean, and says about him that, 'Manannán lived on in folk tradition just as did Donn, Aine, and others' (McNeil, 1962, p. 168). Unlike other mythic figures who survived in folklore, Manannán's later depictions and stories seem to have stayed reasonably true to his earlier personality and appearances, so that he retains a clear continuity from the earliest mythic depictions to the more recent folklore (MacQuarrie, 1997). One may even suggest that Manannán in pop-culture, while clearly departing from the cultural folklore, retains more of a core character that is in keeping with his older depictions than many other figures from Celtic mythology have.

Modern Folklore

John O'Donovan's Letters from Londonderry, written in 1834, includes an array of folklore relating to Manannán. O'Donovan, who describes the god as 'a fairy' and suggests he was a human who had been 'deified or demonified', relates that Manannán has changed his partonomic from mac Lir to McEleer. His Manannán is deeply patriotic, concerned with Ireland's independence, and also worried about fitting into the modern world (MacQuarrie, 1997). O'Donovan shares a folktale, supposedly from the time of Saint Columba, wherein the saint had a maidservant who broke a cup which Manannán repaired with his magic; sensing the repair the saint was angered and berated the maid at which point Manannán appeared and declared the saint's rudeness meant he would leave Ireland.

O'Donovan is uncertain where Manannán resides in the nineteenth century, alternately suggesting inland in Derry, in the waves offshore, or on the Isle of Man.

Fiona MacLeod[1] aka William Sharp was a writer in the nineteenth century who wrote poetry and stories which took, in some cases, a great deal of creative license with the original mythology. Manannán is called 'Manan' in MacLeod/Sharp's work which has him as the brother of Brighid, as well as her lover, who goes missing and who Brighid must search for. She eventually finds him in Iceland and woos him back, returning his blessing and protection to the seas (Williams, 2016). MacLeod/Sharp's re-envisioning of Manannán and Brighid may represent one of the more extreme deviations from the older material and seems to show echoes of Norse myth, particularly later Victorian tales of Freya searching for her lover Od.

Manannán appears in Ella Young's nineteenth-century work *Celtic Wonder Tales* as one of the Tuatha De Danann who first travels with Brighid to earth. Young's work was a visionary re-telling of the older mythology and folklore written through her own poetic lens and includes entirely new stories from the author's imagination. One of these is the first chapter in the book, titled 'The Earth Shapers' which offers Young's vision of what an Irish creation story may have been. Many people in more recent years have mistaken Young's work for genuinely older original mythology and several of her ideas have, in places, become accepted as such. Here we'll look at a sample of the ways Manannán appears in Young's work.

In *Celtic Wonder Tales* the Tuatha De Danann are living in the 'Land of the Living Heart' when Brighid begins singing a song she hears from the earth. The group decides to go and see what is going on there, and they bring their four treasures with them. Once in the chthonic place that is the primordial earth they begin to bring life and creation, but Manannán, there called Mananaun, sees dangerous spirits lurking at the edges of their creation. He draws one of the four treasures, the sword of light, and sweeps it forward creating the sea and driving the dangerous beings back with a wave. He swung the sword a second time giving colour to the ocean and creating another wave, and a third time creating a white-capped wave-like crystal. These three sword sweeps were the three waves of Manannán, beyond which the dangerous beings dwelled, but inside which the Tuatha De Danann lived safely.

In a later chapter, 'How the Son of the Gabhaun Saor Shortened the Road', Manannán appears again in the guise of an old man. The Gabhaun Saor's son is seeking the answer to a problem and runs across Manannán disguised as a frail old man apparently trying to spread out wool across the ground. Seeking to help, the son approachesand realizes the man is actually the God of the sea and the wool is actually the white ocean waves. Nonetheless, Manannán is grateful that he stopped to offer assistance and tells him to take some of the 'wool'; when he does so the sea foam he grabs turns to wool in his hand. This later helps the son when he is being held by the Fomorians, as he divides the wool and uses it to call forth light into the darkness and two cloaks the colour of the sea which hide the son and his father from sight. When they manage their escape they find Manannán has sent his magical coracle, Wave Sweeper, to rescue them; it carried them as swift as thought to safety across the ocean.

Manannán appears as well in the chapter 'The Cow of Plenty', again in disguise as an old man, this time using his magical boat as a ferry. He brings Dian Cecht's son Cian over to Balor's land to retrieve a halter for Goibhniu's cow, making a deal with him along the way that Cian will give him half of whatever he returns with excluding the halter. He also aids Cian by granting him the ability to open any lock and by changing cloaks with him so that he wears Manannán's cloak of invisibility. Cian goes on to serve Balor in exchange for the halter, sneaking into Balor's daughter Ethniu's locked room while he is there, and beginning an affair with her. Eventually a child is born of this union (the god Lugh), and Ethniu gives Cian the halter and the baby and tells him to flee the island. At the shore, Cian finds the old man – Manannán in disguise – waiting for him and makes good his escape. The man asks for what Cian promised, but Cian says all he has is the halter which he cannot give and the baby which he will not divide. To pay what he owes, he agrees to give the infant to the boatman. When he hands over the baby, the boatman transforms into a beautiful man and Cian realizes that it is Manannán who will now be Lugh's foster father.

Young's work is imaginative and varies from older mythology but in many ways she stayed true to the spirit of Manannán as a trickster who would travel in disguise and as a deity who would aid others in achieving their ends. She also kept the idea of Manannán as a God of the Sea and keeper of treasures.

Manannán in Modern Druidism

In my experience Manannán is not widely acknowledged in modern witchcraft or Wicca, but he has claimed a place to some degree in modern Druidry. One reason for this may be his connection to magic and enchantment. Another reason may be that the Féth Fiadha is also sometimes called the Ceo Draoichta, or druidic mist, and it would seem natural to draw a connection between the teacher of this magic and Druidism more generally.

Some neo-Druids see Manannán as the keeper of the gates between our world and the Otherworld and call on him to open the way between the worlds. In Ar nDraoicht Fein, one of America's largest Druidic organizations, for example, I have heard

Manannán referred to as the Gatekeeper deity and know a variety of people who call on him in that capacity.

Pop-Culture Manannán

Modern myths and folklore are not the only places that we see Manannán appearing; he also shows up in pop-culture in different ways. This can mean everything from children's movies to video games. Below I will include a list of some of these pop-culture appearances:

Ulysses – The James Joyce work features Manannán showing up at one point clad in a druidic mantle, covered in shells and seaweed, accompanied by eels.

Song of the Sea – A 2014 animated film focused heavily on lore around selkies. Manannán is called 'Mac Lir' here and is the son of Macha, an 'owl witch', who had turned him into a stone island in the ocean because he was overcome with grief. The movie centres on two children, one of whom is half-selkie, who have been taken by their grandmother to the city and are trying to get back home to their father who lives on an island. They run foul of Macha along the way and eventually end up freeing all of the fairies she has turned to stone, including Manannán and herself.

Iron Druid Chronicles – Manannán appears in the series of books by Kevin Hearne.

Saga of Pliocene Exile – A four-book series by Julian May features a character name Minannon the Heretic as part of her Tanu culture; this character is based on or referencing Manannán as the Tanu reference the Tuatha De Danann.

Meredith Gentry Series – By Laurel K. Hamilton, this series, which heavily features Celtic mythology and fairies, includes a character named Barinthus who had been Manannán god of the sea until the fey folk had agreed to give up a large part of their power in order to integrate (to some degree) with the human world.

Nemeton – A modern novel by Christopher Lee Eichenauer; Manannán appears briefly as a minor character.

Deities and Demigods – An expansion book by TSR, publisher of Dungeons and Dragon allows players to worship Manannán as an in-game deity.

King's Quest III – The classic computer game featured Manannán as one of the villains.

Bard's Tale – A video game where Manannán appears as one of the characters who must be defeated by the player.

Manannán's Statue

In Limavady, Derry, there was a famous statue of Manannán that had been created by John Sutton. The statue was of the sea god, six feet tall and dressed much as an Iron Age Celt would have been, standing in the mock up of the front of a coracle with his arms raised towards the ocean on the horizon. In January 2015, the statue was stolen and a wooden cross left in its place bearing a quote from the Bible[2]; the statue had been a popular tourist attraction and there was a public outcry for its return (Fleming, 2015). A month later the original statue was found within 1000 metres of the location it had stood in, but the head was badly damaged in an apparent attempt to, literally, deface the pagan deity (BBC, 2016). The outcry and public interest, however, motivated the borough council to pay for the same sculptor to replace the original work with a replica, and the replica was installed and now stands at the location.

Manannan's Fountain

There is a bronze fountain depicting Manannán in Castlebar, which is somewhat well known and can be found in articles and photographs online. The piece is a sculpture by Peter Grant and features Manannán riding in a vehicle pulled by two horses through the waves (CITA, 1999). It sits across from a hotel and is illuminated at night (CITA, 1999).

This is merely a small look at some of the ways that we see Manannán in the modern world, in everything from modern myths to artwork. While this can only be a sample of how the deity is found today in various cultural expressions, it should give the reader an idea of both the scope of possibilities as well as the pervasiveness of Manannán. While we might not expect to find the Irish god of the sea in video games or role playing games, there he is, just as he plays a role in works of fiction. Manannán is easy, perhaps, to overlook in a world full of other distractions but nonetheless he is there all around us in pop-culture and in new retellings of older stories.

Manannán in My Life

I remember when the statue of Manannán in Derry was stolen. The story received a lot of coverage because the statue had been created by someone connected to a popular television series and was itself a famous tourist spot. As a pagan it was a difficult story to hear about, coming within a year of the defacement with paint of the Lia Fail at Teamhair. While the initial reports of the statue's theft, of course, offered no explanation for why it had been stolen, it was hard not to feel like it was an attack on paganism in a more general sense. There was a lot of debate online about the wooden cross and Bible verse that was left in the statue's place and whether that was a genuine commentary or a red herring, and there was also a lot of disturbing (to me) support for the statue's removal by some people since it was an Irish pagan deity.

When the statue was found with its face so badly damaged it seemed to reinforce the initial message that was left. For those of us who honour the pagan gods of Ireland it was insult to injury. This was quickly followed by a very real concern that the statue which could not be repaired would not be replaced. In fairness, replacing the statue was an expensive proposition and one that the local council could not easily afford, and the discussion about not replacing it had little to do with Manannán himself and more to do with who would pay for it and the risk of the statue being taken again.

And then something really beautiful to see happened. On social media there was talk of how people – all sorts of people, pagan and non-pagan – could help fund a new statue. There was discussion of crowd funding and donation pages, and even of people sending money directly to the closest town. People were even asking about the possibility of small replica statues and whether the profit from those could fund the new full-size statue. It was beautiful to see people across all sorts of demographics coming together and trying to find solutions, to return this symbol, this deity to his former place.

Eventually, the decision was made to replace the original with a new identical statue made by the same sculptor, paid for by the council and all of this discussion became moot.

But it didn't change the experience for me of seeing first the worst, and then the best that could be in people. It reminded me that there will always be people in the world who seek to destroy what they cannot subjugate … and that there will always be people who seek to heal what is broken.

Endnotes

1. Fiona MacLeod was the pen name for the writer William Sharp who wrote material relating to Celtic culture under both names. Sharp wrote a great deal of material under his own name and also under his female pseudonym, with 'Fiona MacLeod' being presented during his lifetime as a real person distinct from Sharp, a fiction that he went to extreme lengths to maintain. There has been a great deal of modern speculation about Sharp and his creation of MacLeod, his motives, and dedication to the deception. Readers wishing to know more may consider The William Sharp 'Fiona MacLeod' Archive on the University of London website here https://www.ies. sas.ac.uk/research-projects-archives/william-sharp-fiona-macleod-archive

2. Specifically Exodus 20:3 'You shall have no other Gods before me'.

Chapter 7

Connecting to Manannán

Having taken the last chapter to explore some of the ways that Manannán can still be found in the modern world, now let's look at how modern pagans can seek him out in more active ways. There are a nearly endless selection of ways to connect for those who want to get to know Manannán as more than just a character in myths or a being with many different associations and possessions. Some obvious and simple options would be to go and visit the ocean – to experience his realm in a tangible way – or to visit some of the specific real world locations associated with him, like Caiseal Mhanannáin in Roscommon or Barrule on the Isle of Man. However, those may not be viable options for everyone for many different reasons, so here we will look at some other possibilities that may be more accessible to a wider selection of people.

Altars and Shrines

There is no set rule for what an altar to Manannán could or should look like but there are some themes that are logical for such things. In several sources rushes are mentioned as offerings for him, so it could be safely assumed that rushes were historically sacred to him (O hOgain, 2006). The sea and waters were also strongly associated with him, and it said in the story of Oirbsiu that when he died a lake burst forth from his grave. He is also strongly associated with horses and apples. Any of these things could be incorporated into altars for Manannán. What focus a Manannán altar would have would depend on which aspect of Manannán a person is looking at, because although we may automatically default to sea and shoreline imagery, he is of course far more diverse than that. As with any altar or shrine, however, you can use whatever you like to decorate it from images and statues to candles, objects you feel are significant, offering bowls, incense holders, magical tools, divination tools, or things that are purely decorative. Below, I'll provide a few examples to illustrate options but a person has a lot of freedom in how they choose to create a sacred space in their home for him.

Altar to Manannán, son of the sea: blue or wave patterned cloth, blue or white candles, picture or artwork of Manannán in a boat, seashells for decoration, large shell for an offering bowl.

Altar to Manannán as king of the Tuatha Dé Danann: mat of reeds, gold or purple candles, pillar stone or small cairn representing the king's authority, symbols of earth, sea, and sky representing the three realms.

Altar to Manannán, god of magic: white cloth, image of Manannán wearing cloak, magical tools such as wands or candles. A crane bag if you have made one for yourself.

Altar to Manannán as advisor: single white candle, divination tools that you are comfortable using, offering bowl.

For those who are unable, for any reason, to have a permanent altar or shrine space, setting up a temporary space may be an option. If even a temporary space isn't possible there are still a few possibilities. You could set aside a small area that isn't a formal altar or shrine per se but where you could collect objects related to Manannán or that remind you of him such as ocean imagery, shells, model boats, or the like. If even that isn't possible you could visualize the same, creating a kind of mental altar or shrine that you can visit whenever you need to.

Offerings

There are a variety of things that could be given to Manannán as offerings. Looking at the mythology, we see stories of reeds or rushes laid out before him, meaning that they could be a good offering to him. He is also associated with apples and I have had success giving both red and green apples to him. As with any of the Irish gods, it is also generally safe to offer baked goods like breads as well as dairy products, especially milk, cream, and butter.

Some choose to offer alcohol to him and what kind would be a personal preference. I tend to favour ales for Manannán, but other people may have their own approaches to what he likes. I have also, in my own practice, found that he is accepting of good, clean fresh water, so I will often give that.

Meditation to Meet Manannán

A guided meditation can be a good way to start to reach out to Manannán. Even if you have limited or no experience with meditation, it's fairly simple to do and should be safe. You can memorize the meditation script and then run through it yourself, record yourself reading it and then play it back while meditating, or have a friend read it to you. If you want to do this meditation just find a quiet time and place, sit or lay comfortably, and run through the script I'll include below.

It doesn't have to be done perfectly and you should try to be open to the possibility of things going a bit off script: you may have no experience at all and need to do the meditation several times or you might find that your actual experience in the meditation doesn't follow the pre-written story. That's fine. The only thing you should watch for is anything coming up in the meditation that is upsetting or frightening. If at any time you feel unsafe or want to stop, picture a door appearing in front of you, see yourself opening it and immediately being back in your own body awake.

To do the meditation make sure you have enough time undisturbed. Get into a comfortable position and begin.

Relax and feel the ground below you. Feel yourself solid on the earth. Breathe in slowly. Breathe out. In. And out. See yourself surrounded by bright white light and know that you are perfectly safe and protected. Breathe in slowly and deeply and feel the light filling you. Breathe out.

The white light starts to fade around you and you become aware that you are sitting in a green hillside. The sky is blue above you. The air is warm and there is a slight, gentle breeze against your skin. You can hear waves breaking on rocks nearby and smell saltwater and seaweed on the breeze.

You follow the sounds of the waves, down the hillside and up a small ridge. As you reach the top of the next hill you see the rocky shoreline below you and the vast expanse of the ocean spreading out to the horizon. You move down near the edge of the water, finding a comfortable place to rest out of reach of the waves. This is a peaceful place and you sit and enjoy the feel of the warm sun on your skin and rhythmic sound of the waves close by.

After a time you glance up and see a figure moving towards you across the shifting ocean. It is a man, his blonde hair is held back by a golden band and he is dressed in a white shirt and dark blue pants with a cloak around his shoulders that looks like it is made out of the waves themselves. He is walking across the water as easily as if it were dry land and when he sees you watching him he smiles at you. His expression is both kind and friendly. You recognize him as Manannán mac Lir.

He arrives on the shore and steps from wave to sand, still smiling. He greets you by name and then joins you where you are, turning to admire the ocean he just journeyed across. As you stand together you have the opportunity to tell him anything you want to or ask him questions and he gives you any messages he has for you (leave time here for discussion).

When all has been said that needs to be said, Manannán steps away, back towards the water. As he turns to leave, he reminds you that you may always seek his presence there at the shore, although he makes no promises that he will always be free to appear. Then with a final smile he gestures at the waves and a dark grey horse emerges from the water to stand at the edge of the strand. He mounts bareback and the pair race across the water, quickly disappearing from sight.

You sit for another moment, the white crests of the breaking waves looking like horses playing on the sand, then, you turn to leave as well. You make your way back up the hill, leaving the ocean behind you. You head up the second hill, back to the spot where you first arrived. You can still hear the waves and smell the sea, but all you see around you is green hill and blue sky. The sun is warm and the breeze is cool and you feel peaceful and content. Closing your eyes, the green fades and then is consumed by white light which gets brighter and brighter.

Breathe in slowly. Breathe out. Again, feel the earth solidly beneath you. Feel yourself solidly within your own body. Breathe in. Out. Shift your weight, move your body, wiggle fingers and toes. When you feel ready open your eyes.

After the meditation write down any experiences you have had.

A Midsummer Ritual to Manannán

Since midsummer was Manannán's special holiday and the day when people would pay 'rent' to him, those who seek to honour him today can certainly celebrate midsummer especially for him. I'm going to include the outline of a basic Midsummer ritual one could use, and I am keeping it as non-denominational as possible. Feel free to tailor this to suit your own personal approach as much as you need to.

What you will need:

Altar space,
Reeds (if possible),
Alternate offerings if you can't have reeds,
An altar bowl or plate,
A representation of Manannán (image, statue, etc.).

Find a quiet place where you feel connected to Manannán, indoors or outdoors. Ideally this should be somewhere at least semi-private where you won't be disturbed. Set up a small altar as you see fit, perhaps based on some of the examples above; otherwise a simple clear space with an offering bowl or plate and something representing Manannán will suffice.

Create ritual space however you usually would.

Focus on Manannán. Say:

I invoke Manannán, God of the sea
King of the Otherworld, King of the aos sidhe
Who protects those who seek shelter with him
Who guides those who seek his counsel
Foster father of Gods, Kings, and heroes
I invite you here to join me in my ritual
As I seek to honour you on midsummer
Longest day and shortest night
Manannán, Mighty warrior and druid,
Be with me now.

When you feel as if Manannán is present with you, pick up the offering you have brought for him. Say:

I give you these reeds (or ale, or milk, fresh water etc.)
As people have paid their due to you
Since time immemorial
I pay you homage with this offering
In respect for your power
In appreciation for your guidance
In acknowledgement of your presence
May your blessing be on my life
On this day and from this day
Throughout the year to come
(Place the offering.)
Let it be so.

After the offering is made take a few minutes to contemplate the energy around you and look for omens. If you want to include anything else in your ritual do so now.

When you are ready to bid farewell to Manannán say:

Manannán, god of the sea
Rider of Sea-foam
Bearer of the Answerer
Keeper of the Crane Bag
Thank you for your presence
May my offerings be accepted
May your blessing be on my life
And my I remember always
The wisdom of your stories
And the power of your lessons
Thank you, Manannán.

This is a very simple approach to ritual. You can easily make this more complicated or add to it whatever you feel you would need to, including perhaps divination of some sort.

Prayer to Manannán as Psychopomp

Death is always difficult for the living to come to terms with, although it is said that to die to this world is to be born into the Otherworld. One thing we, as modern pagans, need more of is prayers for the dying, to help the soul move on and to comfort the living left behind.

This is a blessing from the Carmina Gadelica to be said at death. I have modernized it and made it more pagan. This could work equally well as something said to a dying person as they pass or as something said to those who are grieving during a funeral or memorial service.

Soul Peace 53:

Since we know the soul is immortal –
At the time of yielding the life,
At the time of pouring the sweat,
At the time of offering the life,
At the time of shedding the blood,

At the time of balancing the beam,
At the time of severing the breath,
At the time of losing the soul,
Peace upon the soul's journey;
As it returns to the land from whence it came,
Peace upon the soul's journey,
As it returns from whence it came.
And may Manannan, gentle and kindly,
Lord of the waves and guide across worlds,
Take possession of the beloved soul,
And shield it home,
Oh! Where it may rest and be reborn again.

Invocation to Manannán

Manannán son of Lir
Whose horses are the breaking waves
Whose cattle are the innumerable fish
Whose fertile plains are the ocean waters
Manannan of the cloak
Manannan of the feast of youth
Manannan of the wise counsel
Son of the sea, Lord of the strand
I call to you.

Prayer to Manannán

Manannán, Lord of the fishful oceans,
Who brings the concealing mists around us
And parts them again to reveal hidden truths
Manannán, God of the endless tides,
Who sees a bountiful plain where we see water
Whose horses are the white crested waves
Manannán, wave-rider, magic worker, counsel-giver
We honour your presence in our lives, in the song of the
    pounding sea,

And we call to you to help us find our way as we sail through uncertainty.

Manannán in My Life

An important lesson I have learned when it comes to Manannán is that he isn't just a multi-faceted deity, he is a being who will relate to us in the ways that we most need to relate to him. I think that this is why in the myths he appeared in certain guises to Cormac, or Fionn, or Caintigern. And in the modern world, I believe this is why people tend to strongly view him in specific ways, whether that is as a god of the sea or magic worker, as an old man or as a handsome warrior. All deities can be fluid in this way, but with Manannán this fluidity isn't just a part of who he is it is an essential characteristic. He comes to each of us in the form and aspect we most need yet is always the same Manannán.

To me, while he will always be a god of the sea, he is the premier lord of the Otherworld, a kind of high-king of the Good People. Many Otherworldly realms are said to be his including the most well known in Irish mythology, but more than that, he reveals the Otherworld to mortals. He brings people there to learn and give them important gifts. And he is so vitally connected to the sidhe – the fairy mounds – that it is Manannán who brought the Tuatha Dé Danann into them and taught them how to live there and how to thrive among the aos sidhe.

One of the basic ways that I incorporate Manannán into my regular practice relates to his role as king of the Otherworld. The main focus of my personal spirituality relates to working with and connecting to the Daoine Sidhe. For me, even when I am not working with Manannán directly, I am acknowledging his place in the hierarchy that runs the Otherworld. Because to me he is always and ultimately the king of the Otherworld before and beyond everything else.

Conclusion

Manannán is a complicated and complex deity but hopefully this small book has helped give the reader a better idea of his history and his mythology across the years, from his earliest appearances in Irish mythology to his place in pop-culture. Times change, dominant religions change, but Manannán remains.

One of the most interesting things about Manannán is the way that he has endured throughout the centuries and adapted across cultural changes. His true origins may be lost to time with some scholars theorizing that he arrived in Ireland from elsewhere, went from there to Wales, and possibly back again to Ireland, while others believe that he began in Ireland and moved outward from there over time. Whatever the truth is, his ambiguous origins create a rich tapestry of mythology and folklore that extends between Ireland, Wales, Scotland, and the Isle of Man.

In the Irish mythology we can see him evolving over time from a liminal figure who gives essential gifts and advice, to an Otherworldly being who shows up in the mortal world to father kings, and finally to an ambiguous and mysterious character, often ill-dressed or unpleasant in appearance, who acts to both help and hinder heroes and lords. As contradictory as the sea, he is a deity of truth and truthfulness yet he is often connected to or involved in illicit love affairs. He is a king but often appears as the crudest of people; beautiful, he can seem grotesque. He is a deity of the waves and open sea but runs faster than the wind and wins races against horses and men over land. A renowned warrior with a multitude of magical weapons and armour, he chooses in the Manx folklore not to fight but uses magical skill and enchantment to frighten away enemies.

As we seek to understand Manannán we must set aside the idea of simple or easy expectations. Instead we must sit back and contemplate the entirety of his mythology and folklore, the good and the bad – or as he says in the story of the Ceithearnach Caoilraibhach, the sweet and the sour – and be willing to embrace that such contradiction is a part of his nature.

Those who seek the Irish god of the sea will find him easily but understanding him may be the work of a lifetime.

Appendix 1

Glossary and Pronunciation Guide

I am often asked to include a pronunciation guide in my books as well as a guide to the English names for the Irish myths. I thought for this text I would try to accommodate that. Below, I will include a glossary of the names of the myths in the Irish as I include them throughout this book, followed by the most common English name for the same story. Then I will have a small section with some of the deity names and other Irish language names included in the book and how they would be pronounced in modern Irish.

Glossary of Story Names

Lebor Gabala Erenn – The Book of the Takings of Ireland

Serglige Con Culain – The Wasting-Sickness of Cu Chulainn

Tochmarc Etaine – The Wooing of Etain

Tochmarc Luaine – The Wooing of Luaine

Cóir Anmann – The Fitness of Names

Altram Tige Dá Medar – Fosterage of the House of Two Milk-Pails

Ceithearnach Caoilraibhach – The Kern in the Striped Pants

Echtra Bhodaigh an Chóta Lachtna – Adventures of the Churl in the Dull-brown Coat

Echtra Airt meic Chuind – Adventures of Art Son of Conn

Echtra Cormaic meic Airt – Adventures of Cormac Son of Art

Dunaire Finn – Poems of Fionn

Imramm Brain meic Ferbail – Voyage of Bran Son of Ferbal

Compert Mongáin – Conception of Mongan

Oidheadh Chloinne Lir – Fate of the Children of Lir

Toruigheacht Diarmada agus Grainne – The Pursuit of Diarmuid and Grainne

Abridged Pronunciation Guide

Aengus – Ayn-guhs

Áine – Awn-yuh

Aoife – EE-fuh

Aos Sidhe – ace shee

Corr Bolg – core boh-lug

Emhain Abhlac – Ehw-ahn Av-lak

Enbhar – Ehn-var

Fand – Fahnd with the a as in father

Féth fíadha – Fay Fee-ah

Fuamnach – Fuhmna(ch) with the ch like in loch

Lugh – Loo

Manannán – Mah-nah-nawn

Midhir – Me'er

Sidhe – shee

Tír na nÓg – Teer nuh Nowg

Tír Tairngire – Teer Tahrn-gih-reh

Bibliography

BBC (2016) Manannán mac Lir: sea god statue back on Binevenagh mountain. Retrieved from http://www.bbc.com/news/uk-northern-ireland-foyle-west-35679046

Beveridge, J., (2014) Children into Swans: fairy tales and the pagan imagination

Bromwich, R., (2006) Trioedd Ynys Prydein

CITA (1999) The Mall Fountain. Retrieved from http://www.castlebar.ie/fountain.htm

Cross, T., and Slover, H., (1936) Ancient Irish Tales

Curley, D., (2013) Rathcroghan Monuments Spotlight No. 2 – Cashelmanannan: a monument with a complex story to tell. Retrieved from http://cruachanai.blogspot.com/2013/12/rathcroghan-monuments-spotlight-no-2.html

Daimler, M., (2018) Compert Mongan

--- (2018) Sanas Cormaic la.82

--- (2016) Treasure of the Tuatha De Danann: A Dual Language Pocket Book

Dobs, M., (1929) The Fosterage of the House of Two Milk Pails; Zeitchrift für Celtische Philologie vol. 18 (1929-30)

Douglas, M., (1917) Mychurachan

Ellis, P., (1987). A Dictionary of Irish Mythology

Evans-Wentz, W., (1911) The Fairy Faith in Celtic Countries

Fleming, J., (2015) Manannán Mac Lir Statue Discovered Dumped in Countryside. Belfast Telegraph. Retrieved from https://www.belfasttelegraph.co.uk/news/northern-ireland/manannan-mac-lir-statue-is-discovered-dumped-in-countryside-31012423.html

Green, T., (2007) Concepts of Arthur

Jones, M., (2003) Manannán mac Lir Retrieved from http://www.maryjones.us/jce/manannan.html

Leahy, A., (1906) Heroic Romances of Ireland, volume II

Logainm.ie (n.d.) Caiseal Mhanannán. Retrieved from https://

www.logainm.ie/ga/1410349?s=Caiseal+Mhanann%C3%A1in

Macalister, R., (1944) Lebor Gabala Erenn, vol. 4

MacCoitir, N., (2012) Irish Wild Plants

MacKillop, J., (1996) A Dictionary of Celtic Mythology

Macneill, E., (2015) Dunaire Finn, The Book of the Lays of Fionn, vol. 1

MacQuarrie, C., (1997) The Waves of Manannan: A Study of The Literary Representations of Manannan Mac Lir from 'Immram Brain' (c. 700) To 'Finnegans Wake' (1939)

Manannan mac Lir (2018) Manx Fairy Tales: Manannan mac Lir Retrieved from http://www.isleofman.com/welcome/history/mythology-and-folklore/manx-fairy-tales/manannan-mac-lir/

McNeill, M., (1962) The Festival of Lughnasa

Monaghan, P., (2004). The Encyclopedia of Celtic Myth and Folklore

Meyer, K., (1895) The Voyage of Bran Son of Ferbal

Moore, A., (1891) The Folk-lore of the Isle of Man

Morrison, S., (1911) Manx Fairy Tales

O hOgain, D., (2006). The Lore of Ireland

O'Curry, E., (2009) The Sickbed of Cu Chulainn and the Only Jealousy of Emer

O'Grady, S., (1892) Silva Gadelica

Parker, W., (2003) The Four Branches of the Mabinogi Retrieved from http://www.mabinogi.net/index.html

Rhys, T., (1881) The Hibbert Lectures: Lectures on the Origins and Growth of Religion

Richardson, M., (2017) The Manx Crisis of 1916 and the Emergence of Mona Douglas in the Nationalist Movement

Sanas Cormaic (n.d.) Early Irish Glossaries Database. Retrieved from http://www.asnc.cam.ac.uk/irishglossaries/

Sims-Williams, P., (2011) Irish Influence on Medieval Welsh Literature

Smyth, D., (1988) A Guide to Irish Mythology

Stokes, W., (1891) *The Irish Ordeals, Cormac's Adventures in the Land of Promise, and the Decision as to Cormac's Sword,* Irische Texte mit Wortebuch vol. 3

--- (1903) *The Wooing of Luaine and the Death of Athirne; Tochmarc Luaine 7 Aidedh Aithairne Andso*: Yellow Book of Lecan, Book of Ballymote. Review Celtique 24

Todd, J., (1892). Leabhar Breathnach Annso Sis

Williams, M., (2016) Ireland's Immortals: A History of the Gods of Irish Myth

Young, E., (1910) Celtic Wonder Tales

MOON

BOOKS

PAGANISM & SHAMANISM

What is Paganism? A religion, a spirituality, an alternative belief system, nature worship? You can find support for all these definitions (and many more) in dictionaries, encyclopaedias, and text books of religion, but subscribe to any one and the truth will evade you. Above all Paganism is a creative pursuit, an encounter with reality, an exploration of meaning and an expression of the soul. Druids, Heathens, Wiccans and others, all contribute their insights and literary riches to the Pagan tradition. Moon Books invites you to begin or to deepen your own encounter, right here, right now.

If you have enjoyed this book, why not tell other readers by posting a review on your preferred book site. Recent bestsellers from Moon Books are:

Journey to the Dark Goddess
How to Return to Your Soul
Jane Meredith
Discover the powerful secrets of the Dark Goddess and transform your depression, grief and pain into healing and integration.
Paperback: 978-1-84694-677-6 ebook: 978-1-78099-223-5

Shamanic Reiki

Expanded Ways of Working with Universal Life Force Energy
Llyn Roberts, Robert Levy
Shamanism and Reiki are each powerful ways of healing; together, their power multiplies. *Shamanic Reiki* introduces techniques to help healers and Reiki practitioners tap ancient healing wisdom.
Paperback: 978-1-84694-037-8 ebook: 978-1-84694-650-9

Pagan Portals – The Awen Alone

Walking the Path of the Solitary Druid
Joanna van der Hoeven
An introductory guide for the solitary Druid, *The Awen Alone* will accompany you as you explore, and seek out your own place within the natural world.
Paperback: 978-1-78279-547-6 ebook: 978-1-78279-546-9

A Kitchen Witch's World of Magical Herbs & Plants

Rachel Patterson
A journey into the magical world of herbs and plants, filled with magical uses, folklore, history and practical magic. By popular writer, blogger and kitchen witch, Tansy Firedragon.
Paperback: 978-1-78279-621-3 ebook: 978-1-78279-620-6

Medicine for the Soul

The Complete Book of Shamanic Healing
Ross Heaven
All you will ever need to know about shamanic healing and how to become your own shaman...
Paperback: 978-1-78099-419-2 ebook: 978-1-78099-420-8

Shaman Pathways – The Druid Shaman
Exploring the Celtic Otherworld
Danu Forest
A practical guide to Celtic shamanism with exercises and
techniques as well as traditional lore for exploring the Celtic
Otherworld.
Paperback: 978-1-78099-615-8 ebook: 978-1-78099-616-5

Traditional Witchcraft for the Woods and Forests
A Witch's Guide to the Woodland with Guided Meditations and
Pathworking
Melusine Draco
A Witch's guide to walking alone in the woods, with guided
meditations and pathworking.
Paperback: 978-1-84694-803-9 ebook: 978-1-84694-804-6

Wild Earth, Wild Soul
A Manual for an Ecstatic Culture
Bill Pfeiffer
Imagine a nature-based culture so alive and so connected,
spreading like wildfire. This book is the first flame…
Paperback: 978-1-78099-187-0 ebook: 978-1-78099-188-7

Naming the Goddess
Trevor Greenfield
Naming the Goddess is written by over eighty adherents and
scholars of Goddess and Goddess Spirituality.
Paperback: 978-1-78279-476-9 ebook: 978-1-78279-475-2

Shapeshifting into Higher Consciousness
Heal and Transform Yourself and Our World with Ancient
Shamanic and Modern Methods
Llyn Roberts
Ancient and modern methods that you can use every day to
transform yourself and make a positive difference in the world.
Paperback: 978-1-84694-843-5 ebook: 978-1-84694-844-2

Readers of ebooks can buy or view any of these bestsellers by
clicking on the live link in the title. Most titles are published in
paperback and as an ebook. Paperbacks are available in traditional
bookshops. Both print and ebook formats are available online.

Find more titles and sign up to our readers' newsletter at
http://www.johnhuntpublishing.com/paganism
Follow us on Facebook at https://www.facebook.com/MoonBooks
and Twitter at https://twitter.com/MoonBooksJHP

RAND 1700 Main Street, PO Box 2138 Santa Monica, CA 90407-2138

ERRATA

July 7, 2003

**PUBLICATIONS
DEPARTMENT**

To: Recipients of *Phase Transition in Korea-U.S. Science and Technology Relations*, by Caroline Wagner, Anny Wong, SungHo Lee and Irene Brahmakulam (MR-1644-ROK)

From: Publications Department

Begin at page iii. Replace third sentence in first paragraph with the following:

The study was supported by the Korea-U.S. Science Cooperation Center (KUSCO), and the research was conducted in close cooperation with the Science and Technology Policy Institute of Korea (STEPI).